THE ESSENCE OF

COMPUTING PROJECTS
A STUDENT'S GUIDE

THE ESSENCE OF COMPUTING SERIES

Published Titles
The Essence of Artificial Intelligence
The Essence of C for Electronic Engineers
The Essence of Compilers
The Essence of Databases
The Essence of Discrete Mathematics
The Essence of Human–Computer Interaction
The Essence of Java Programming
The Essence of Logic
The Essence of Neural Networks
The Essence of Professional Issues in Computing
The Essence of Program Design
The Essence of Programming Using C++
The Essence of Structured Systems Analysis Techniques
The Essence of Z

Forthcoming Titles
The Essence of Distributed Systems
The Essence of Expert Systems
The Essence of Information Technology

THE ESSENCE OF

COMPUTING PROJECTS
A STUDENT'S GUIDE

Christian W. Dawson
Loughborough University

Prentice Hall

An imprint of Pearson Education

Harlow, England · London · New York · Reading, Massachusetts · San Francisco
Toronto · Don Mills, Ontario · Sydney · Tokyo · Singapore · Hong Kong · Seoul
Taipei · Cape Town · Madrid · Mexico City · Amsterdam · Munich · Paris · Milan

Pearson Education Limited
Edinburgh Gate
Harlow
Essex CM20 2JE
England
and Associated Companies throughout the world

Visit us on the World Wide Web at:
http://www.pearsoneduc.com

© Pearson Education Limited 2000

The right of Christian W. Dawson to be identified as author of this Work has been asserted by him in accordance with the Copyright, Designs and Patents Act 1988.

All rights reserved. No part of this publication may be reproduced, stored in a retrieval system, or transmitted, in any form, or by any means, electronic, mechanical, photocopying, recording or otherwise, without either the prior written permission of the publisher or a licence permitting restricted copying in the United Kingdom issued by the Copyright Licensing Agency Ltd, 90 Tottenham Court Road, London W1P 0LP.

Many of the designations used by manufacturers and sellers to distinguish their products are claimed as trademarks. Addison Education Ltd has made every attempt to supply trademark information about manufacturers and their products mentioned in this book. A list of the trademark designations and their owners appears below.

First published 2000

Typeset in 10 on 12 pt Times by 25
Printed and bound in Great Britain by Biddles Ltd, *www.biddles.co.uk*

Library of Congress Cataloging-in-Publication Data

Dawson, Christian W.
 The essence of computing projects : a student's
 guide / Christian W. Dawson.
   p. cm.
  Includes bibliographical references.
  ISBN 0–13–021972–X
  1. Computer science—Research Handbooks,
manuals, etc. I. Title.
QA76.27.D39 2000
004′.07′22—dc21   99–29612
                                                    CIP

British Library Cataloguing-in-Publication Data

A catalogue record for this book is available from
the British Library

ISBN: 0–13–021972–X

1 2 3 4 5   03 02 01 00

Trademark Notice
Microsoft, PowerPoint and Windows are registered trademarks of Microsoft Corporation. Reference Manager is a registered trademark of the Institute for Scientific Information. Post-it Notes is a trademark of 3M.

10 9 8 7 6 5 4 3 2

04 03 02 01 00

For my father

Contents

Preface xi

1 Introduction: What are computing projects? *1*
   1.1 Introduction *1*
   1.2 What is research? *2*
   1.3 The research process *6*
   1.4 Classifying research *10*
   1.5 What are projects? *14*
   1.6 Summary *17*
   1.7 Exercises *18*

Part I: Setting your project's foundation *19*

2 Choosing a project and writing a proposal *21*
   2.1 Introduction *21*
   2.2 Choosing a project *21*
   2.3 Preparing a project proposal *28*
   2.4 Choosing your supervisor *35*
   2.5 Summary *36*
   2.6 Exercises *36*

3 Project planning *37*
   3.1 Introduction *37*
   3.2 Project definition *38*
   3.3 Project planning *40*
   3.4 Summary *55*
   3.5 Further reading *56*
   3.6 Exercises *56*

Part II: Conducting your project *57*

4 Literature searching and literature reviews *59*
   4.1 Introduction *59*
   4.2 The literature survey process *63*

4.3 Literature searching *65*
4.4 Managing information *73*
4.5 Critical evaluation *75*
4.6 Writing literature reviews *77*
4.7 Summary *80*
4.8 Further reading *81*

5 Doing your project *82*
5.1 Introduction *82*
5.2 Dealing with problems *85*
5.3 Managing your time *88*
5.4 Using your supervisor *96*
5.5 Working in teams *99*
5.6 Summary *104*
5.7 Further reading *104*
5.8 Exercises *105*

Part III: Presenting your project *107*

6 Presenting your project in written form *109*
6.1 Introduction *109*
6.2 Writing and structuring reports *110*
6.3 Writing abstracts *117*
6.4 Data presentation *119*
6.5 Referencing material and avoiding plagiarism *130*
6.6 Documenting software *137*
6.7 Summary *140*
6.8 Further reading *141*
6.9 Exercises *141*

7 Presentation skills *142*
7.1 Introduction *142*
7.2 Oral presentations *143*
7.3 Demonstrating software *152*
7.4 Viva voce examinations *155*
7.5 Summary *158*
7.6 Further reading *159*

8 Final considerations *160*
8.1 Introduction *160*
8.2 Taking your project further *160*
8.3 Additional topics *163*
8.4 British Computer Society exemption and accreditation *164*
8.5 The future *167*

8.6 Summary *169*
8.7 Exercises *170*

Bibliography 171
Index 174

Preface

Projects are a major component of virtually all undergraduate and postgraduate computing and information systems courses within universities. They require students to draw on a number of separate but highly important skills: surveying literature, report writing, documenting software, presentational skills, time management, project management skills and so on. For students to excel in all of these areas is a major accomplishment, yet it is something that academic institutions have come to expect as part of the independent learning process.

While there are books available that cover *some* of these topics in great detail, there are none that draw *all* these skills together and which are aimed specifically at students on computing courses of one kind or another. This text fills this gap and provides a foundation in the skills needed by both undergraduate and postgraduate students to complete academic computing projects successfully.

This book is structured in a chronological fashion so that the main stages through which computing projects progress are discussed in sequence. It begins with a general introduction to research and computing projects before being split into the following three main sections:

Setting your project's foundation. This section covers the skills you will need
  during the initial stages of your computing project. It covers topics such as
  how to choose a project, how to write a project proposal and how to plan
  for your project's accomplishment.

Conducting your project. This section covers the skills you will need while
  you are actually working on your project – from doing your literature
  survey to managing your time and any information and data that you
  collect, as well as how to liaise effectively with your supervisor.

Presenting your project. The final stage of your project will be to present it as
  a written report and, possibly, with an oral presentation. This section
  covers the skills you will need to present your project in the best light and
  to the best of your abilities.

The content of this book is based on course material from three research methods modules taught at the University of Derby. One of these modules has been developed to prepare undergraduate students for their final year projects in computer studies and information systems. Another module is aimed at specialist MSc and MSc conversion students, and additional material has been developed from a research methods module that is taught to PhD students university-wide.

I would like to take this opportunity to thank those people who have helped and supported me with writing this book. This includes colleagues who have provided me with technical advice and, perhaps more importantly, the encouragement and support I have received from both my wife, Sarah, and my mother.

Christian Dawson
March 1999

The publishers wish to thank the following for permission to reproduce the following copyright material:

IAHS Press for text on pages 78–80 from Dawson, C.W. and Wilby, R. (1998) An artificial neural network approach to rainfall runoff modelling, *Hydrological Sciences Journal*, 43(1), 47–66.

Open University Press for Figure 1.2 from Orna, E. and Stevens, G, (1995) *Managing Information for Research* (Open University Press: Buckingham).

CHAPTER 1
Introduction: What are computing projects?

Aims
To introduce academic computing projects.

Learning objectives
When you have completed this chapter, you should be able to:

- discuss what research means;
- understand the research process;
- classify research and understand the different research methods that are available;
- understand what projects are and, specifically, the different types of academic projects that there are in computing.

1.1 Introduction

Pursuing an undergraduate or postgraduate project within academia is not the same as performing one within industry. As a student on a computing degree course of one kind or another you will be expected to look at things much more critically and more deeply than you would elsewhere.

In industry, for example, your line manager might ask you to develop a piece of software to solve a particular problem or improve productivity in a particular area – a database, a production control system or whatever. You could write this program satisfactorily and install it within a few months and everyone would be happy. However, although this program might be perfectly adequate and work very well in practice, academically this project would be lacking.

Why is this the case? Academic projects should provide evidence of a much deeper understanding of what you are doing. They require some form of justification and contextualisation. You are not expected to do merely what you are told to do, but you are expected to develop your own thoughts, arguments, ideas and concepts. You are expected to question things and look at things in new ways and from new angles. Merely 'turning the handle', or doing what you are told, does not lead to intellectual discovery and contributions to world thinking. As a degree student you are expected to *think*.

This 'deeper' understanding of situations, problems and events is supported by your *research* skills. These skills are vitally important within academic projects. This chapter will begin, therefore, by exploring what is meant by research before looking in more detail at computing projects themselves.

1.2 What is research?

> The good researcher is not 'one who knows the right answers' but 'one who is struggling to find out what the right questions might be'.
>
> Phillips and Pugh (1994: 48)

1.2.1 A definition

Research is defined by the Higher Education Funding Council for England as '*original* investigation undertaken in order to *gain knowledge* and understanding' (HEFCE 1998). There are three key terms within this definition that have been italicised for emphasis: *original*, *gain* and *knowledge*. These points are discussed in turn in the following subsections.

1.2.2 Originality

There is no point in repeating the work of others and discovering or producing what is already known. Originality, quite simply put, is doing something or producing something that has not been done before. While this remains a relatively simplistic idea of the term, it is important to discuss how originality relates to projects. What can *you* do that is original? What type of things can *you* produce that are original?

You can be original in two ways. First, you can be original in the way you do things — for example, doing something someone has done before but using a different technique or approach. Second, you can be original by producing or developing something that has not been produced before.

In terms of originality in the way you do things, Cryer (1996: 146) identifies a number of areas in which your project can be original:

- *Tools, techniques, procedures and methods.* You may apply new tools and techniques to alternative problems, or try new procedures and methods in contexts where they have not been applied before. Whether these investigations prove successful or not you will still be doing something that is original and discovering why these approaches are suitable in certain circumstances or not.

- *Exploring the unknown.* Although rare, you may investigate a field that no one has thought to investigate before. Recent discoveries in scientific fields may open up many new possibilities and unexplored avenues of research that you can pursue.
- *Exploring the unanticipated.* Although you may investigate a field of research that has been looked at many times before, you may come across unexpected results or exciting new directions that have not been explored. Investigating these 'side tracks' may prove fruitful but care must be taken as they may lead to dead ends. You might also be able to contribute to these fields by further developing original work.

  Exploring a field that has already been investigated does not necessarily fail to be original. You may be able to improve on something that already exists, provide a new perspective or interpretation, or produce a unique in-depth study of that field that has not been available before.
- *The use of data.* You can interpret data in different ways, use them in new ways or apply them in alternative areas that have not yet been investigated.

In terms of your project's outcomes, Cryer (1996: 147) identifies originality from the perspective of the results themselves and, also, any original by-products of the research. Thus, original outcomes might include a new product, a new theory, a new model or a new method. Where the intended outcomes are not achieved, by-products might still represent originality – for example, an understanding of why a particular experiment failed or why a particular technique did not work in a new area.

1.2.3 **Gain**

Gain is, perhaps, an unfortunate term in the HEFCE definition because it does not allude to the fact that research should actually lead to a *contribution* to knowledge. It is all very well performing an exclusive piece of research and learning something new for yourself, but unless you can disseminate this knowledge to others, the results of your research are somewhat wasted. With this in mind the following discussion focuses on the term 'contribute', which gives the much clearer message that research should add to world knowledge so that it is accessible to all and not just yourself.

Figure 1.1 provides an overview of the world's body of knowledge (BOK) and how contributions can be made to it. This BOK represents world understanding, theories, concepts, models, the sciences, the arts and so on. Your own knowledge is shown subsumed within this domain by the shaded region. You can obviously learn things that others already know, shown as expansion to your own knowledge 'cloud'. Likewise, you can make contributions to world knowledge from your research, such as inventions, new theories and so on.

4 INTRODUCTION: WHAT ARE COMPUTING PROJECTS?

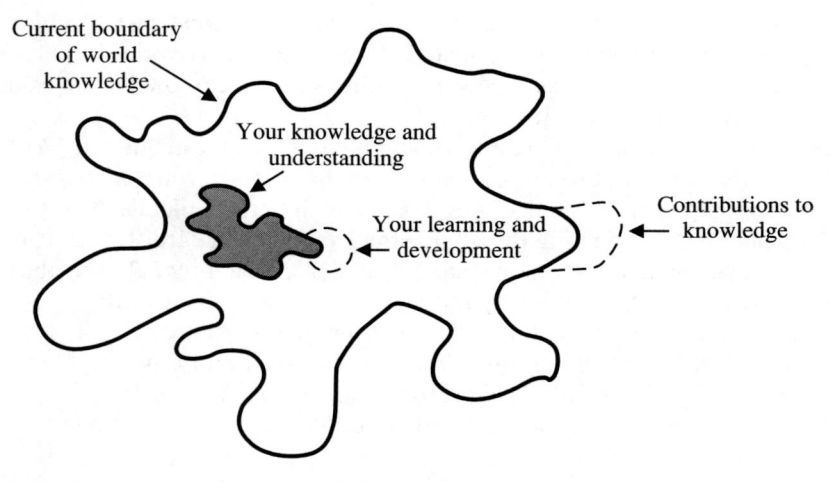

Figure 1.1 *Contributions to knowledge*

These are shown as expansions to the world's BOK by a dashed line. Thus, contribution refers to a sharing of new ideas, theories and results with the rest of the world and expanding what is already known.

1.2.4 **Knowledge**

In order to explain what is meant by knowledge, it will be discussed in terms of a hierarchy consisting of *data, information, knowledge* and *wisdom*. Post and Anderson (1997: 7) identify the meaning of these terms as:

- *Data*. Data are the factual elements that describe objects or events. They represent the raw numbers and raw text that you gather from your investigations. For example, as part of your research project, you may need to gather rainfall data from various sites around the country. These data, providing daily rainfall totals at fifty sites, are gathered as raw numbers that mean virtually nothing as they stand.
- *Information*. Information represents data that have been processed in order to provide you with some insight into their meaning. In other words, the data have been analysed, summarised and processed into a more understandable and useful format. In this form information can be passed to other people; for example, in books, articles, recordings, speech and so on (Orna and Stevens 1995: 36).

  Converting your rainfall data into information may lead to graphs summarising monthly totals, charts presenting seasonal fluctuations and text or tables summarising average daily rainfall at different sites. In these formats the data have some meaning and you now have some insight into what these data represent.

- *Knowledge.* Knowledge is your higher level understanding of things. While information provides you with an idea of the 'what' (i.e. what is happening in the real world), knowledge represents your understanding of the 'why'. Knowledge is your personal interpretation of what you gain from information as rules, patterns, decisions, models, ideas and so on. According to Orna and Stevens (1995: 35), knowledge represents the 'results of experience organized and stored inside each individual's own mind'.

  While your information about UK rainfall provided you with an overview of *what* was happening to weather in Britain over a period of time, knowledge represents your understanding of *why* rainfall might have changed during this period. For example, your knowledge would be your understanding of why rainfall had increased in particular parts of the country since 1900.

- *Wisdom.* Wisdom represents your ability to put your knowledge into practice. It represents your ability to apply your skills and experiences to create new knowledge and adapt to different situations.

  With respect to the rainfall example, wisdom would represent your ability to predict likely changes to rainfall and climate in the future or enable you to understand why rain falls at particular levels in an entirely different part of the world.

One more category that is worth mentioning here is *theory*. While data, information, knowledge and wisdom represent a relatively 'firm' understanding of what is going on and how things can be applied, theory represents ideas, opinions and suppositions based on your observations of the world. A theory is not necessarily true but, at the moment, it represents the best explanation of what you observe.

Although knowledge has been defined from a personal viewpoint, *world knowledge* can be defined along much the same lines. In this case world knowledge relates to world understanding, wisdom and interpretation by everybody and everything that is recorded or documented somewhere and somehow.

Collecting data and information on their own is termed 'intelligence-gathering' by Phillips and Pugh (1994: 46). These data are used to answer what Phillips and Pugh term the 'what?' questions: What is happening in the world? What don't we know? What can we find out?

Research, however, must go beyond merely gathering data and describing what you see. It must make a contribution to *knowledge*. It looks for 'explanations, relationships, comparisons, predictions, generalisations and theories'. Research thus addresses what Phillips and Pugh term the 'why?' questions: Why do things happen the way they do? Why is the situation the way it is? and so on. While data and information on their own can only answer the 'what?', knowledge and wisdom address the 'why?'.

1.2.5 Summary

Now that the three main aspects of research have been looked at in detail, one other definition of research is presented to see if it encapsulates the essence of the term. As an example take Sharp and Howard's (1996: 7) definition of research:

> seeking through *methodical processes* to *add* to one's own body of *knowledge* and, hopefully, to that of others, by the *discovery* of *non-trivial facts* and *insights*.

Once again, the important terms within this definition have been italicised; some of them relate directly to those that have been discussed already. 'Add', for example, relates to the discussion of 'contribution', and 'discovery' appears to imply some form of 'originality'. The term 'hopefully' is, perhaps, misplaced as you would expect to make a contribution from your research. 'Non-trivial facts' and 'insights' relate to 'knowledge' and 'wisdom', not data or information.

One element that this definition contributes that the earlier definition from the HEFCE did not, is the idea of a 'methodical process'. This identifies the fact that research is not something that is done in an *ad hoc* manner but is something that is planned and pursued in a considered way. Thus, the process of performing research, which is discussed in the following section, is *methodical*.

Drawing these points together results in the following succinct definition of research, which encapsulates all the elements discussed so far – consideration, originality, contribution and knowledge:

> *Research is a considered activity which aims to make an original contribution to knowledge.*

1.3 The research process

1.3.1 Overview

One thing that the above definition of research recognised is that research must be a considered activity. In other words, your research activity should not be performed as and when you feel like it, but should follow a recognised process. Blaxter *et al.* (1996: 7) identify four common views of the research process; these will be referred to as *sequential, generalised, circulatory* and *evolutionary*:

- *Sequential*. The sequential process is the simplest view of all. In this process a series of activities are performed one after another as a 'fixed, linear series of stages'.

An example of such a process is the systematic process model of Sharp and Howard (1996: 15). This process consists of seven unique, sequential steps:

- identify the broad area of study;
- select a research topic;
- decide on an approach;
- plan how you will perform the research;
- gather data and information;
- analyse and interpret these data;
- present the results and findings.

Although this model appears entirely sequential, Sharp and Howard (1996: 15) do admit that repetition and cycles may take place during this process. However, how and when this repetition takes place is not explicitly identified. Another, perhaps simpler, example of a sequential research process is that defined by Greenfield (1996: 7). Greenfield breaks the research process into four steps:

- review the field, i.e. perform a literature survey;
- build a theory based on your understanding and interpretations of the field;
- test the theory: does it work?;
- reflect and integrate, i.e. update your ideas based on your 'tests' and contribute your new-found knowledge to others.

- *Generalised*. The generalised research process is identical to the sequential process in that activities are performed one after the other in a defined sequence. However, the generalised model recognises that not all stages are applicable and some steps may require performing in different ways depending on the nature of the research. Thus, the generalised model identifies alternative routes that may be taken at different stages depending on the nature and outcomes of the research. An example of such a model is that of Kane (1985: 13, cited by Blaxter *et al*. 1996: 8).
- *Circulatory*. The circulatory approach recognises that any research that you perform is really part of a continuous cycle of discovery and investigation. Quite often research will uncover more questions than it answers and, hence, the research process can begin again by attempting to answer these new-found questions. Experiences of research might lead you to revisit or reinterpret earlier stages of your work (Blaxter *et al*. 1996: 7). The circulatory interpretation also permits the research process to be joined at any point and recognises that the process is never ending.

An example of a circulatory process is Rudestam and Newton's

Research Wheel (1992: 5), which suggests a 'recursive cycle of steps that are repeated over time'.
- *Evolutionary.* The evolutionary concept takes the circulatory interpretation one stage further and recognises that research must evolve and change over time, not necessarily following a defined circulatory pattern or repeating the same forms of analysis and interpretation that were performed before. The outcomes of each evolution impact on later ones to a greater or lesser extent.

Perhaps one of the more appropriate examples of the research process is that defined by Orna and Stevens (1995: 11). They define a process that is circulatory at the top level and evolutionary within the main search/investigation stage of the process. Figure 1.2 is an adapted interpretation of this model.

Figure 1.2 shows a circulatory research process that begins in the top left-hand corner with a definition of your search. Orna and Stevens (1995: 11) identify this search definition as an attempt to answer the following questions:

- What am I looking for?
- Why am I looking for it?
- How shall I set about it?
- Where shall I start looking?

Following on from this stage you begin your *evolutionary* investigation of the chosen research area. This investigation will take place within the current boundaries of world knowledge as you search through, digest and evaluate material that is available. This search/investigation is not clear cut and will

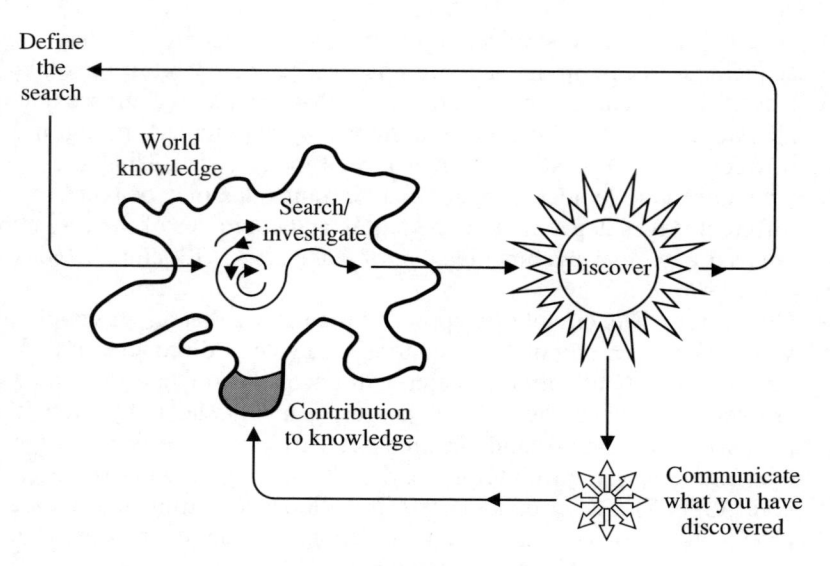

Figure 1.2 *The real research process*
Source: Adapted and reproduced with kind permission from Orna and Stevens (1995).

evolve over time. It will take time for your ideas to mature, you may find yourself pursuing dead ends, and you might create more questions than answers. Eventually, however, your diligence will hopefully pay off and you will discover something of value.

This discovery must then be disseminated to others through your reports, presentations, articles and discussions. There is no point in keeping discoveries to yourself as to do so ignores a fundamental purpose of the research process – that of disseminating your new-found ideas and results to others. Through this communication you are able to make a contribution to world knowledge and understanding, shown by the shaded area in Figure 1.2.

However, although you may have discovered something of value, and contributed this to world knowledge, the research process might be only just beginning. These discoveries might lead to new questions, new avenues of research and so on. Thus, the research cycle is entered once again as you redefine your search and continue your voyage of discovery.

1.3.2 *Intellectual discovery*

While the research process can be represented by a model of one kind or another, your own reasoning processes and intellectual discoveries are often much more complex and personal. When you are looking for questions to answer and answers to those questions, you will often follow a complex process of *inductive* and *deductive* reasoning.

- *Inductive reasoning*. You start with your observations of the world and come to general conclusions about it. In other words, you build models and theories based on your interpretation of the world. Clearly, this interpretation will depend on the data and information you can draw from the world, the subject or problem you are studying and, importantly, what you already know and believe.

  The knowledge that you can obtain from what you are studying is referred to as *epistemology* (Cornford and Smithson 1996: 39). You can either draw general conclusions from what you observe and from what you are studying and apply them to other things (*positivism*), or you can only induce knowledge unique to yourself and the particular situation under study (*anti-positivism*).
- *Deductive reasoning*. You start with your knowledge and understanding of the world and predict likely observations within it, even though you might not have encountered them before.

  Deductive reasoning is affected by your theory of reality, your own personal understanding of the world and your underlying assumptions about what you are investigating. This is referred to as *ontology*. Different people might deduce different things as their understanding differs from your own and they see things in different ways.

To solve complex problems you might need to follow a complex chain of inductive and deductive reasoning. Knowledge, which was discussed earlier, is what you derive from inductive reasoning. In other words, you build your ideas, models, theories and understanding based on your inductive reasoning about the world. Wisdom, on the other hand, is evident from your abilities of deductive reasoning – applying what you know to other situations and problems you have not yet encountered.

There is more to intellectual discovery than inductive and deductive reasoning alone. If you are having difficulty solving a problem, two interesting methods of intellectual discovery listed by Greenfield (1996: 5) that might help are:

> The method of **Pappus**: assume the problem is solved and calculate backwards.
> The method of **Terullus**: assume a solution is impossible and try to prove why.

In addition, Greenfield also suggests trying techniques such as:

- *Random guesses*. A similar technique to brainstorming, whereby you can try to solve a problem by generating a number of potential solutions at random. Hopefully one of them will make sense and work.
- *Analogy*. Is the problem similar to anything else that already has a solution or explanation?
- *Inversion*. Try to look at things from the opposite angle. For example, instead of asking 'which computer language should I use?' ask 'why shouldn't I use Pascal?'.
- *Partition*. Break the problem or situation down into smaller, more manageable and understandable parts.

It is also worth considering where you are heading with your research before you spend several months pursuing it. For example, quite often research students will get an idea for their investigation and pursue it enthusiastically. However, when they finally obtain the 'answer' they realise that it was of little value in the first place. Try to think of where you are going, assume you have obtained the answer already, and ask yourself 'so what use is this to me?'.

1.4 Classifying research

1.4.1 Introduction

Research can be classified from three different perspectives: its *field*, its *approach* and its *nature*. These three categories are adapted from the four categories discussed by Sharp and Howard (1996: 11) and Herbert (1990: 1). These authors identify an additional category called *purpose*. However, as the purpose of research is arguably to contribute to knowledge, the way that research achieves this contribution has been identified here subsumed within its *nature*.

- *Field*. The field of research is 'little more than a labelling device that enables groups of researchers with similar interests to be identified' (Sharp and Howard 1996). For example, in computing you might identify research fields in areas such as information systems, artificial intelligence, software engineering and so on.
- *Approach*. Approach represents the research methods that are employed as part of the research process – for example, case study, experiment, survey and so on. These methods are discussed in more detail in the following section.
- *Nature*. The type of contribution that research makes to knowledge depends upon its nature. Sharp and Howard (1996: 13) identify three levels that can be used to classify the nature of research:
  - Level 1: pure theoretical development;
  - Level 2: research that reviews and assesses pure theory and evaluates its potential for practical application;
  - Level 3: applied research that has some practical application or outcome.

The nature of research can also be identified according to the following common classifications which are adapted from Sharp and Howard (1996: 13), Herbert (1990: 1) and Saunders *et al.* (1997: 78–79):

- Pure theory: developing theories to explain things without necessarily linking them to practice. This can be based on your own inductive reasoning which leads you to make conclusions and theories about the world as you see it.
- Descriptive studies: reviewing and evaluating existing theory and knowledge in a field or describing particular situations or events. This might include testing existing theories, describing the state of the art, or looking for limits in previous generalisations.
- Exploratory studies: exploring a situation or a problem. These studies are useful for finding out 'what is happening; to seek new insights; to ask questions and to assess phenomena in a new light' (Robson 1993: 42, cited by Saunders *et al.* 1997: 78–79). Exploratory studies can be performed through literature searches, open questionnaires and interviews. These studies can start out by exploring particularly broad areas, concepts and ideas before focusing in and narrowing down to specifics as the research progresses. The process is thus an iterative and flexible one that seeks new information and ideas.
- Explanatory studies: explaining or clarifying something or some phenomena and identifying the relationships between things.

- Causal studies: assessing the effects that one or more variables have on another. The independent variables are those that might be having an influence on the dependent variable in which you are interested. In these studies you would manipulate the independent variables and monitor changes to the dependent variable. For example, does the size of software product (independent variable) affect how difficult it is to maintain (dependent variable which is measured in some way)?

   In these studies it is important to ensure that extraneous factors do not influence your results. For example, software size appears to be influencing maintainability but, in fact, maintainability might be due to a range of other factors you were unaware of and did not control.
- Resolving a problem with a novel solution and/or improving something in one way or another.
- Developing or constructing something novel.

1.4.2 Research methods

While techniques for sampling, data gathering, interviewing and so on are beyond the intended scope of this book, it is useful to take a brief look at some of the more widely recognised research methods that are available. Whether you use these methods at all, or decide to combine them in one way or another, will clearly depend on the nature of your project. Four of the most common research methods that you might use are *action research*, *experiment*, *case study* and *survey*.

Action research
Action research involves 'the carefully documented (and monitored) study of an attempt by you ... to actively solve a problem and/or change a situation' (Herbert 1990: 29). It involves working on a specific problem or project with a subject or, more usually, an organisation and evaluating the results. This method is used to gain 'a greater understanding and improvement of practice *over a period of time*' (Bell 1993: 8). With action research you must ensure that you do not become too obsessed with completing the action itself and neglect the real reason for doing it – that is, evaluating it as part of your academic project.

Experiment
Experiment involves an investigation of causal relationships using tests controlled by yourself. Quite often quasi-experimental research will have to be performed due to problems of insufficient access to samples, ethical issues and so on. According to Saunders *et al.* (1997: 75), experiments typically involve:

- defining a theoretical hypothesis;
- selecting samples from known populations;

- allocating samples to different experimental conditions;
- introducing planned changes to one or more variables;
- measuring a small number of variables;
- controlling all other variables.

Case study

A case study is 'an in-depth exploration of one situation' (Cornford and Smithson 1996: 49). It involves the investigation of a particular situation, problem, company or group of companies. This investigation can be performed directly, for example, by interviews, observation and so on, or indirectly by studying company reports or company documentation. For more information on case study research you can refer to texts such as Yin (1989) and Easton (1992), which are entire books devoted to this issue.

Survey

This is usually undertaken through the use of questionnaires or interviews. 'It allows the collection of a large amount of data from a sizable population in a highly economical way' (Saunders *et al.* 1997: 76). As part of a survey you might have to identify samples, select sample sizes, design questionnaires and define interviews as appropriate. Fowler (1995) and Czaja and Blair (1996) are two texts that cover this topic in detail.

Research methods can also be classified according to their 'time frame'. In other words, does the study that has been performed result in a snapshot of what you have observed or do your data provide an insight into events over a *period of time*? A snapshot of a situation or event is referred to as a *cross-sectional* study. A long-term picture, on the other hand, in which data are gathered continually over a period of time, is called a *longitudinal* study. Which kind of study you use will depend on the nature of your research and what you hope to achieve. For more information on these kinds of study refer to texts such as Saunders *et al.* (1997: 77) and Cornford and Smithson (1996: 48).

1.4.3 *What is good research?*

You should now have an idea of what research is about and how to classify it, but what is meant by *good* research? Phillips and Pugh (1994: 47) identify three characteristics of good research:

- *Open minds*. You should work with an 'open system of thought'. Be open minded to the questions posed. 'Conventional wisdom and accepted doctrine ... may turn out to be inadequate.'
- *Critical analysis*. Examine data critically. Are these figures correct? Have they been affected in some way? What do these data *really* mean? Are alternative data available? Can these data be interpreted differently?

- *Generalisations*. Researchers generalise and specify limits on the generalisations they identify. Generalisation allows research to be interpreted and applied to a wide variety of situations. However, researchers must know the limitations of these generalisations. Generalisations stem from your own wisdom and evolve from your deductive reasoning, which leads you to develop ideas about things you have not encountered before, with certain caveats.

Failure to apply these characteristics perpetuates the status quo – everything remains unchallenged and stays the same. Without an open mind to things, without a critical eye and without an ability to generalise your understanding to different things, you will not make a contribution to knowledge. This is, after all, the main aim of your research.

1.5 What are projects?

1.5.1 Introduction

Although you should now understand what is meant by research and the research process, it is still necessary to identify what is meant by projects, computing projects in particular, and how research fits within this context. This section begins by discussing what is meant by projects in a more general sense first.

A project has been defined as 'something which has a beginning and an end' (Barnes 1989, cited by Turner 1993: 4). Unfortunately, this rather broad definition does not encapsulate the underlying purpose of projects, which is to bring about some form of beneficial change. This change takes you from a current existing situation to a desired situation sometime in the future. This can be represented by the *Meliorist model* shown in Figure 1.3. In this figure a project is represented by a set of actions that you perform. A project thus enables you to move from one situation to another. Your movement towards the desired situation might stem from a dissatisfaction with your current situation, a lure towards a situation which appears more satisfactory, or some combination of the two.

The desirable situation in this case represents some form of contribution to knowledge – perhaps representing the development of a new tool, technique, discovery and so on. The term 'contribution' in this context necessarily implies the uniqueness of the project and the novelty of its outcomes.

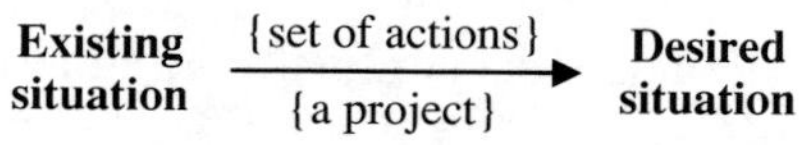

Existing situation →{set of actions}/{a project}→ **Desired situation**

Figure 1.3 *The Meliorist model*

While project managers are concerned with other aspects of projects, such as their complexity, constraints, organisational aspects and so on, as an individual you will only be concerned with the change that your project brings about – that is, the contribution that it will make. This simplistic interpretation of projects will do for now.

So far projects have been identified as having a beginning and an end: bringing about a beneficial change by making some kind of contribution. Looking more specifically at computing projects in particular, you need to see what kind of contributions these projects can make.

Computing projects come in all different shapes and sizes as the field they are drawn from is immense. However, these days it is more widely recognised, within academic institutions, that computing projects need to do more than, for example, develop a piece of software. The project that you pursue must involve an element of research, it must justify its context, and evaluate and discuss its results. Merely developing a tool or algorithm with no evaluation or contextualisation may well be acceptable in industry, where commercial solutions are required. However, within the academic world, this is not the case and, depending on the nature of your project, it will have to contain an element of research to a greater or lesser extent.

The computing project that you embark upon gives *you* an opportunity to make your *own* contribution. There is little point in doing a project that merely regurgitates the work of others. Your own thoughts, ideas and developments *are* important, and these are the things that people reading your report are interested in. It is through your project that you will develop, not only your own skills, but also the ideas and work of others. The level of contribution made by undergraduate and postgraduate projects is looked at in more detail in Section 4.1.

The following section introduces the different kinds of project that you are likely to encounter within the field of computing. In each of these cases it has been identified how these projects make some kind of academic contribution. They do not merely follow a simplistic project process to develop a product at the end of the day.

1.5.2 *Computing project types*

As a guideline, projects in computing tend to fall into one of the following five categories:

- *Research-based project*: 'many good dissertations do no more than review systematically, and impose some structure on, a field of interest' (Sharp and Howard 1996: 25). A research-based project involves a thorough investigation of a particular area, improving your understanding of that area, identifying strengths and weaknesses within the field and acknowledging areas suitable for further development and

investigation. This kind of project will involve some form of literature search and review and would be suitable for undergraduate or taught Masters courses.
- *Development project*: this category includes the development not only of software and hardware systems, but also of process models, methods and algorithms. It may well require you to include evaluation, requirements documentation, designs, analyses and fully documented test results, along with user manuals or guides.

    Depending on the nature of your course the focus for a development project may vary. For example, for software engineering courses, more emphasis may be placed on the development and evaluation of a piece of software following particular process models that generate interim evaluatory documentation. Information systems courses may require you to focus more on the development of broader systems using 4GLs, CASE tools and/or database systems. In this case human–computer interaction (HCI), customer issues and requirements capture problems may be more your focus.

    Whichever kind of development project you tackle it is unlikely that the development of a product would be acceptable on its own. You would normally be expected to include a critical evaluation of the product as well as the development process used. Critical evaluation emphasises the distinction between the academic quality of your work and technical ability alone.
- *Evaluation project*: this category encompasses all projects that involve some form of evaluation as their main focus. A project of this nature might involve an evaluation of several approaches to a particular problem, an evaluation of two or more programming languages (applied in different contexts or to different problems), an evaluation of an implementation process within a particular industry, an evaluation of different user interfaces, an evaluation of a particular concept, and so on. Projects in this category may well include case studies as a vehicle for evaluating the issue under consideration.
- *Industry-based project*: this is simply an industry-based project that involves solving a problem within either an organisation or another university department. Care must be taken with these kinds of projects to ensure that they are not 'hijacked' by the sponsor. In other words, your project must not be forced in a direction that the company wishes it to go which is not necessarily suitable for your academic work or your course. You will probably find that an action research method is employed in this kind of project.
- *Problem solving*: this can involve the development of a new technique to solve a problem or might involve improving the efficiency of existing approaches. It might also involve the application of an existing problem solving technique to a new area. In these cases, some form of evaluation

would be expected; for example, did your new approach work well or did you discover reasons why it was unsuitable for problems of this nature?

These categories are not mutually exclusive and you may find that your project draws on approaches that are identified in more than one of them. In addition, the nature of your project will have an effect on the methods you will use to tackle it. The research methods that you might employ within your project were discussed earlier.

1.5.3 Programming in computing projects

It is not necessarily the case that, because you are on a computing course of one kind or another, you will automatically be expected to write a program. Computing is a broad field and encompasses many topics, including information systems, software engineering, knowledge engineering, HCI, data communications, networks, computer systems architecture and so on. Not all of these fields involve programming and to write a program for the sake of it is clearly ill advised.

Sometimes programming is the main emphasis of your project; for example, if you are on a software engineering course. At other times you may need to write a program as a 'vehicle' for testing and demonstrating one thing or another; for example, to test out some ideas, demonstrate a technique or algorithm, or evaluate some HCI concepts.

Whatever the case, as a computing student you will naturally be expected to produce code that is of an acceptable *quality*. Although you may not be expected to produce a fully documented piece of software with test plans, designs, evaluation and so on, any code that you do produce should be satisfactory for your aims. Your supervisor should be able to advise you on the breadth and depth of any software that you produce as part of your project, so make sure that you liaise with him or her closely.

1.6 Summary

- Research is defined as 'a considered activity which aims to make an original contribution to knowledge'.
- The research process can be either *sequential, generalised, circulatory* or *evolutionary*.
- Research can be classified according to its *field, approach* and *nature*. Approaches to research include *case studies, experiments, surveys* and *action research*.
- Computing projects tend to fall into one of the following five

categories: *research based*, *development projects*, *evaluation projects*, *industry based* or *problem solving*.

1.7 **Exercises**

1. Try to formulate your own definition of research and ask yourself what research means to you.
2. Classify your own computing project into one of the categories identified in Section 1.5.2.

PART I

Setting your project's foundation

CHAPTER 2
Choosing a project and writing a proposal

Aims
To introduce techniques for choosing an appropriate project, and to introduce the basics of writing a satisfactory project proposal.

Learning objectives
When you have completed this chapter, you should be able to:

- choose an appropriate project;
- write a project proposal;
- make effective decisions when choosing your project supervisor.

2.1 Introduction

Because the field of computing is extremely diverse, covering a vast range of topic areas, from sociological and management issues to highly technical hardware and software developments, it is not always easy to decide on a suitable project for your degree course. The types of projects that are accepted in different university departments also vary. Some departments may be happy for you to pursue highly technical programming projects (provided they include satisfactory design and implementation), while others require more academic content which emerges from critical evaluation, analyses and literature surveys. Chapter 1 introduced the categories in which computing projects tend to fall: *research based, development projects, evaluation projects, industry based* and *problem solving*. This chapter introduces the skills you will need and some tips for choosing an appropriate computing project for your course. It then discusses ways in which you can present an acceptable proposal for your chosen project and provides some advice on choosing an appropriate supervisor, if this is possible within your institution.

2.2 Choosing a project

This can often be the most difficult stage of all. Just as an artist ponders over a blank canvas, you have to decide on the type of project you would like to pursue over the following six to twelve months. When choosing your project, it is important that:

- You feel you are capable of doing the proposed project in the time available. You must ensure that your project is not overly ambitious and that you have all the relevant skills that are needed. You may like to consider developing new skills or enhancing some existing skills as part of your project but remember to allow time for this.
- You choose a project that interests you. Remember that you will be working on your project for probably six months or more and it is important that you do not become bored and lose motivation during this time.
- Your project has a serious purpose – it has a clear outcome that will be of benefit to someone.
- Your project has a clear outcome (in terms of deliverables) that focuses your work and direction. Without a clear target to aim for you may lose your motivation as your project progresses and may lose your way.
- Your project links in suitably with your degree course. For example, you would not pursue a highly technical electronics-type development on an information systems course or perform a detailed systems analysis project on an artificial intelligence course.
- Your project is of sufficient scope and quality to fit the requirements of your course.
- It is not a personal issue; that is, you may have a subjective view about a topic that might cloud your perspective and influence your results.

There are various techniques and information sources at your disposal to help you choose a suitable project. These can be summarised as:

- *Lecturers'/departmental lists*: sometimes the only source of acceptable project ideas. These project ideas may have been proposed by academic staff in your department, they may be projects proposed by other departments in the university, or they may be small projects that have been requested by local industry.
- *Past projects*: usually your department or university library will hold copies of previous projects. These can provide you with ideas (for example, how you may develop the work further), and they will give you an idea of the scope and amount of work that is expected from you.
- *Talking with colleagues*: your peers can often provide you with a different perspective on ideas you might have. They may highlight shortcomings with your intended project and may suggest alternatives.
- *Reading around subject areas*: if you read books, journals and articles on a topic that interests you, you can often discover areas that authors have identified as requiring further research and development. As you

improve your understanding of the topic area you may identify a gap in the field that you wish to investigate further. Whatever happens, reading around your intended subject area does no harm and it helps you to prepare a solid understanding of the subject on which you will 'build' your project.

- *Clustering*: you might wish to pursue a project in a particular field but are unsure exactly which aspects of the topic upon which to focus. Clustering can help you to identify aspects within a topic area that link together and are worthy of further investigation. Clustering is performed in two stages. First, you should list keywords related to your chosen topic area. Second, once you have exhausted all the words and phrases you can think of, you cluster them together into related groups and patterns. By doing this you will identify specific topics that interest you and form the basis of your intended project.

Clustering can be used to develop *Research Territory Maps* (RTMs), *Relevance Trees* and *Spider Diagrams*. An RTM, sometimes called an *affinity diagram*, shows how topics relate to one another within your chosen field or fields of study. RTMs provide you with your own conceptual model of your research area. They can be enhanced with thicker and thinner connecting lines to emphasise the strength of relationships between subjects. Figure 2.1 provides an example of an

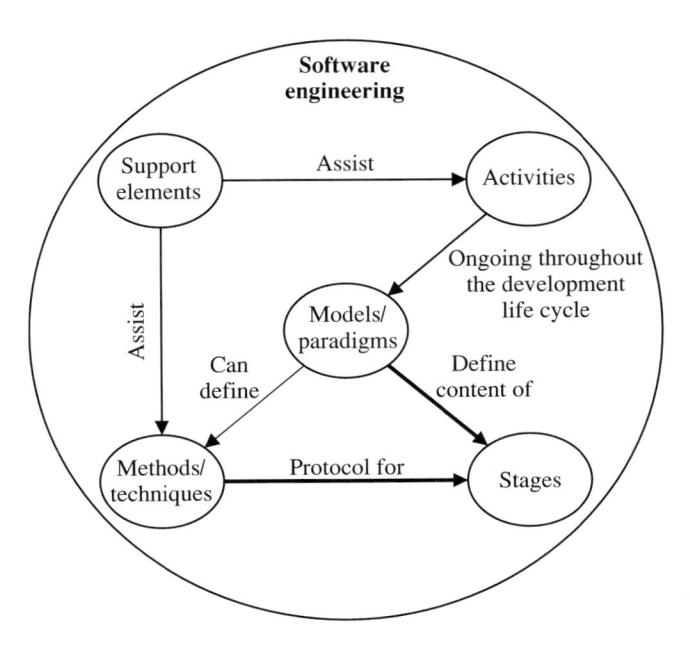

Figure 2.1 A high-level RTM for the field of software engineering

24 CHOOSING A PROJECT AND WRITING A PROPOSAL

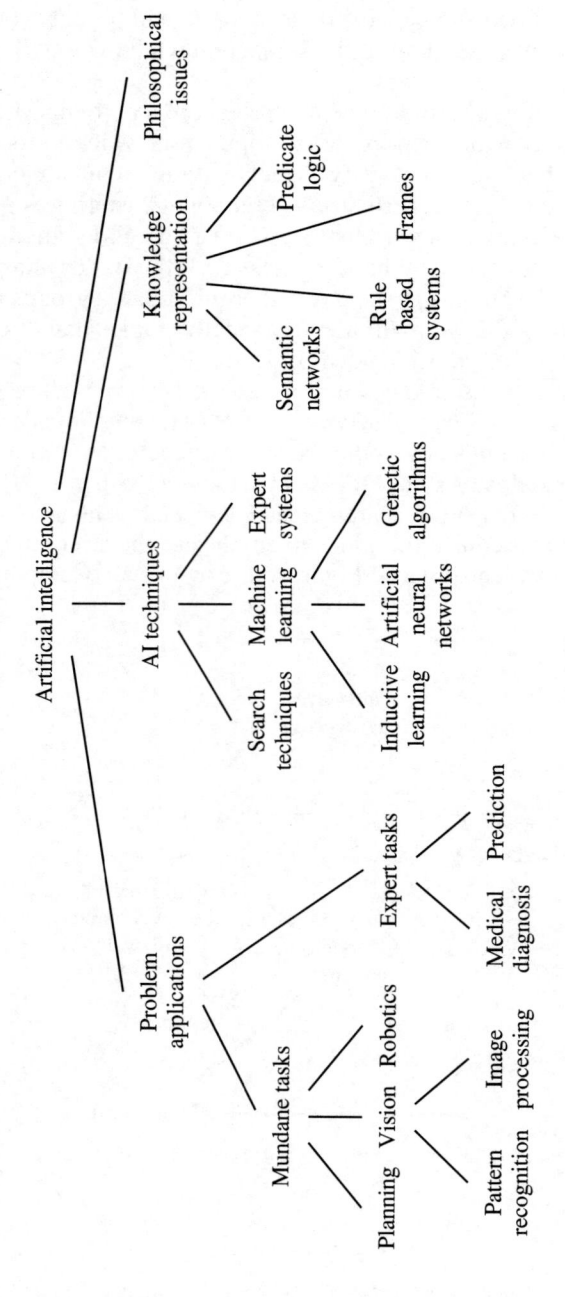

Figure 2.2 *An example relevance tree for the field of artificial intelligence*

RTM – in this case a high-level conceptual map of the field of *software engineering*. These maps help to identify links between related topics and help you to classify and sort any research material that you obtain in your chosen field. RTMs will identify specific topics you might wish to focus on within larger subject areas or, for broader studies, interrelated subjects that are dependent and require investigation.

Relevance trees, discussed in more detail by Sharp and Howard (1996: 33) and Saunders *et al.* (1997: 50), are similar to RTMs in that they try to model your field of study. Where relevance trees differ from RTMs is in their hierarchical structure. While RTMs identify related topics and the links between them, relevance trees break down a particular subject or research question into lower and lower levels of detail, identifying how a subject is composed or identifying the factors affecting a research question posed. RTMs provide a holistic interpretation of the field of study while relevance trees provide a hierarchy of topics that constitute that field of study. An example of a relevance tree for *artificial intelligence* is shown in Figure 2.2.

Another way of structuring your thoughts and identifying how subjects break down is through the use of spider diagrams. These diagrams are similar to RTMs in that they show how topics within a subject area relate together. They are also similar to relevance trees in that they show how topics break down from a central idea, subject or research question. In spider diagrams a central node is used to represent the topic of interest and lines emanating from this node identify how the topic can be organised into its constituent parts. Colours are often used to group ideas and topics together. Figure 2.3 provides a spider diagram interpretation of the field of software engineering. This diagram is adapted from the RTM in Figure 2.1.

Remember that relevance trees, RTMs and spider diagrams are structured by you to represent your *own* interpretation of your chosen subject area. Other people may decompose your subject area into an alternative structure or use different terminology for the same things. You must be aware of these differences so that you are not confused by what appears to be contradictory information which you gather from your literature search. For example, in Figure 2.2, some authors may subsume *Knowledge representation* within *AI techniques* or might disregard *Philosophical issues* entirely, while others may include other topics not identified here.

- *Brainstorming*: if you are really struggling for a project idea, brainstorming can provide the answer. Brainstorming involves 'throwing' any and all the ideas you have down on a piece of paper, in any order and as quickly as possible. You should write anything down, even if it sounds completely irrational, as the brainstorming process

26 CHOOSING A PROJECT AND WRITING A PROPOSAL

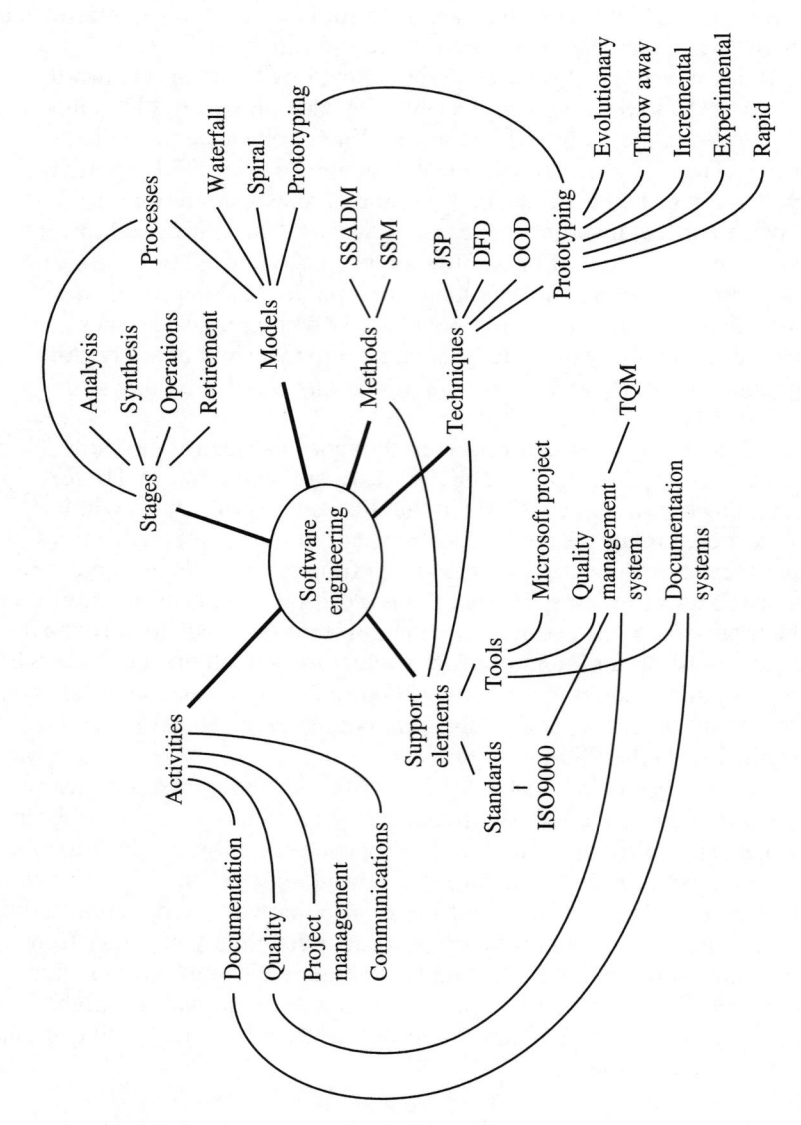

Figure 2.3 *An example spider diagram for the field of software engineering*

should not be stifled. When you have finally exhausted all of your ideas you should look at each one in turn and evaluate and assess it in more depth. What may have sounded ridiculous at first may actually lead to a good project idea; perhaps when viewed from a different angle. You might also like to group your thoughts (using clustering) as this may help to clarify, in your own mind, where your real interests lie. One way to choose between topics is to toss a coin – not to see which way the coin lands but to see how you feel you want the coin to land while it is spinning in the air.
- *Chapter breakdown*: once you have an idea for your project it is a good idea to identify how your project will break down into a number of chapters for the final report. If you have difficulty identifying a number of specific chapters for your final report it may mean that you are unclear about the detail of your project and do not really understand what it is you hope to achieve. Breaking down your project into chapters will also give you an indication of its scope. If you can only identify two or three chapters then maybe your project is not sufficiently broad. Conversely, if you can identify ten or more chapters you may be trying to do too much.

Some additional considerations that should be made when you feel you have chosen your project are:

- *The 'so what?' test* (Herbert 1990: 7). You have decided on your project but 'so what?'. Is the topic meaningful? If you complete the project successfully will it be of value to anybody? What contribution will it make? These are the kinds of questions you should be asking yourself to ensure that you do not pursue something that has no value or worth. Pursuing a meaningless project can lead to poor motivation as your project progresses and you begin to question what is the point of your work.
- *Justification*. Can you explain your project and justify it (the 'so what?' test) in simple terms to the man or woman in the street. If so, you have a good understanding of the subject area and the topic you want to pursue. Note, however, that your explanation may be too technical or too deep for the man or woman in the street to understand but this still means that *you feel* you can explain it in simple terms because the topic is so clear to you.
- *Numerating your understanding*. Can you put a figure on what you know about your chosen subject; for example, 80%? If you are able to numerate your understanding about a topic it means that you have, at least, a concept of that field of study and an awareness of its magnitude. If you have no idea what your understanding is then you have no idea of your subject area's depth or breadth and to undertake a project in this area would be very risky.

This principle was initially presented by Lord Kelvin, who stated:

> When you can measure what you are speaking about and express it in numbers, you know something about it: when you cannot measure it, cannot express it in numbers, your knowledge is of a meagre and unsatisfactory kind. It may be the beginning of knowledge, but you have scarcely in your thought advanced to the stage of science.

This idea is sometimes referred to as *metaknowledge*. This refers to knowledge about knowledge, which means that you have some concept of your own understanding about a particular issue, event or subject. In some ways the wiser people become the more they realise just how little they really know. This is especially true when they place their understanding within the broader context of world knowledge, even though their own expertise in a particular subject may be very deep.

- *Contacts.* Are the contacts you require for your project available, accessible and willing to help; for example, contacts within a local company who have volunteered to help you with a case study? If not, then your project is going to face problems that will need to be dealt with sooner or later.
- *What do you already know?* Orna and Stevens (1995: 29) suggest that another consideration which should be made when identifying your research area is to think about what you already know or have access to that is relevant. This is useful in that it will help you to clarify your strengths and, perhaps, form a foundation for your RTM, relevance tree or spider diagram. In addition, you might also want to identify what you want to *learn* by doing your project – what are your educational objectives? Are there any skills you would like to develop or new techniques you would like to learn? If this is the case, you may like to include a need for these skills within your project to force yourself to learn them.

Using these ideas, sources and approaches will assist you in deciding on your project. However, although you may now have an idea for a project that you feel is of suitable quality and scope for your course, you must now 'sell' it to others with a project proposal.

2.3 **Preparing a project proposal**

2.3.1 **Introduction**

It is normal, in most institutions, for you to prepare a proposal for your project so that it can be assessed for acceptability. Unless you can present an acceptable proposal your project will never even start. It can serve as a contract between you, and your department and project supervisor – but don't expect it to be used against you if you achieve more than you actually intended to do! In many cases projects can, and do, change direction as they proceed, as you become more aware of the topic area and the problem you are investigating. This is acceptable provided that the scope and quality of your project do not become 'watered down' and you are not heading so far away from your initial intentions that the project becomes unrecognisable. If this were the case you would need to obtain permission for significant changes and possibly have to submit a new proposal.

When preparing your proposal there are two golden rules:

- Follow any guidelines precisely. Most institutions have specific information they require; for example, project title, project objectives, hardware required etc. Failure to complete these sections may mean your proposal is rejected without even being read; for example, because you failed to get an academic signature, or did not complete an essential section properly.
- Proofread it thoroughly (and get someone else to check it). Any errors and omissions will appear sloppy and put your commitment and proposed project in a bad light.

There are no universal standards for project proposals although there are particular pieces of information that all proposals should include. This content emerges from your proposal's *implicit content* and *explicit sections*, which are discussed below.

2.3.2 Implicit content

In general, there are four areas that your proposal should address. These areas may not be identified explicitly in the structure of your proposal but they should be addressed implicitly within the proposal's content. They are:

1. Introduction to the subject area. This will provide the reader with an understanding of the field in which your project lies and an idea of where and how your project fits into this field. This aspect will set your project into an overall *context* and will show that it is bound within a recognised field – not an idea that you've had that makes no sense and has no recognisable foundation.
2. Current research in the field. This will emphasise that your project is not based in a field that is out-of-date and that you are aware of current issues within that field of study. It will also imply that you have done some preliminary research into the topic area and are not approaching your project with little background or motivation.
3. Identify a gap. You should be able to identify some aspect of the field that requires further investigation or study. There is no point in

repeating the work of others (unless you are evaluating their approaches) and this component emphasises that the field is not exhausted and is worthy of further investigation.
4. Identify how your work fills the gap. Having identified a gap in the field your proposal should show how your project intends to fill this gap or at least go some way to investigating it further. This will emphasise the *contribution* that your project will make.

2.3.3 **Explicit sections**

Detailed below are the most common sections that project proposals should include. If you are given no guidance as to the content of your project proposal you should include the following three sections as an absolute minimum.

1. Title. This should be clear and concise. Try to avoid using acronyms if possible. Examples of clear and concise titles are:

- 'Evaluation of soft systems methods as analysis tools in small software houses'
- 'Artificial neural networks for software development cost estimation'
- 'Development of process models for graphical software tools'

2. Aims and objectives. Aims identify at the highest level what it is you hope to achieve with your project – what you intend to achieve overall. An aim is a broad statement of intent that identifies your project's purpose. Objectives, on the other hand, identify specific, measurable achievements you hope to make that build towards the ultimate aim of your project. They are more precise than aims as they are 'quantitative and qualitative measures by which completion of the project will be judged' (Turner 1993: 108). They represent major components of your project that direct your work activity (Weiss and Wysocki 1992: 13).

Identifying aims and objectives clarifies, in your own mind and that of the reader, what you specifically hope to achieve with your project. They are also used to assess your project at the end. For example, did you really achieve all that you set out to do? Because of this they should be clear and unambiguous. Chapter 3 discusses aims and objectives further.

An example of aim and objectives is:

Aim:
- To evaluate artificial intelligence techniques for modelling weather patterns.

Objectives:
- To identify and evaluate existing weather pattern modelling techniques;

- To identify artificial intelligence approaches suitable for modelling weather patterns;
- To develop an artificially intelligent system for modelling weather patterns;
- To design and develop an artificial neural network for modelling weather patterns;
- To compare an artificial neural network approach with other artificial intelligence techniques identified and existing approaches to modelling weather patterns.

3. Expected outcomes/deliverables. This section will identify precisely what you intend to submit at the end of the project. It may well identify a written report that covers particular points and makes certain recommendations. A chapter breakdown may be included where appropriate. It can include programs and user documentation and it might include models and algorithms that will be developed to address specific problems. You might also be delivering a functional specification for a piece of software, a prototype or a test plan.

The sections introduced above represent a minimum set that your project proposal should include. Additional sections that proposals can contain, and you might wish to consider including, are:

4. Keywords. Keywords are used to identify the topic areas that your project draws on. They are used by people to see at a glance what subjects your project relates to, which might not be clear from your project's title alone. Libraries and databases also use keywords to help classify material. You might be limited on the number of keywords you can use, for example four or five. Remember that keywords are not necessarily individual words but can be linked words or simple phrases as well; for example, artificial intelligence.

5. Introduction/background/overview. This section would provide an overview of your project and introduce the background work to it. In this section you might wish to include reasons why you feel you are a suitable candidate for performing the project (why you feel you can do it, what skills are required and how you fulfil these requirements), why the topic interests you specifically, and why you chose the project in the first place. This section might also include an introduction to the industry/organisation that is being investigated/evaluated. Overall this section will set the scene of the project for the reader.

6. Related research. This section is used to identify other work, publications and research related to the topic of interest. It will demonstrate that your project is not placed in an academic vacuum but relates to research topics and fields that are currently of interest. Related research can also help to demonstrate your understanding of your topic area to the reader, showing that you are

aware of what is currently happening in the field and are conversant with other topics that impinge upon it.

7. Type of project. You might wish to identify the type of project you are undertaking; for example, research based, development project, evaluation project etc. However, make sure that these terms are recognised and provide more detail if appropriate.

8. Research questions and hypotheses. Your project proposal may also include a research question you intend to investigate and, hopefully, answer to some extent within your project. Computing projects do not necessarily set out to answer particular questions but for some projects a statement of your research question is essential. Examples of research questions are:

- Does the size of an organisation affect its commitment to software quality standards?
- What is the relationship, if any, between software maintainability and coding structure standards?
- Is there an optimum solution to the prediction of software development costs?
- How do large organisations maintain quality standards in the development of internal software?

While research questions on their own are 'open-ended opportunities to satisfy your curiosity' (Rudestam and Newton 1992: 56), they are often linked closely with one or more hypotheses. A hypothesis is 'a tentative proposition which is subject to verification through subsequent investigation' (Verma and Beard 1981: 184, cited by Bell 1993: 18). Although you do not have to define hypotheses alongside a research question, they do present potential 'answers' to the question(s) you have posed and provide definitive statements that will focus your research. Examples of hypotheses that might be investigated, based on the fourth research question posed in the list presented above, are:

Hypothesis 1: Large organisations invariably employ recognised standards to maintain internal software quality.

Hypothesis 2: Large organisations generally have internal quality departments which oversee the implementation of procedures that ensure the quality of internal software.

It is also worth mentioning here the importance of maintaining research *symmetry* with respect to research questions and hypotheses. Research symmetry implies that your 'results will be of similar value whatever you find out' (Gill and Johnson 1991, cited by Saunders *et al.* 1997: 13). With this in mind it is important to realise the implications of the hypotheses you have stated. If they are true you must ask yourself 'so what – was that really worth proving?'. Thus, each hypothesis that you state should have a similar value if proved.

9. Methods. This section will identify the research methods and project methods you will be employing to perform your project. This section should not identify methods that you might be investigating as part of your project, but those methods you are actually using. It might include development methods (for example, SSADM) that you are using as part of a systems development, survey methods for a case study evaluation, and evaluation methods that are used to compare two or more systems. Research methods would include those introduced in Chapter 1, such as action research, case study, survey and experiment.

10. Resource requirements. You might need to identify any resource requirements for your project such as hardware, software and access to particular computers. It may be that you already have access to particular resources and this should be pointed out within this section. Quite clearly, if the resources for your project are not available in your department, or are too expensive to obtain, your project will be unacceptable. However, if you know you need a particular piece of software or hardware you must find out its cost and include this information within this section. A proposal that omits this information may be rejected because the assessor does not know the price or availability of the item, and might assume that it is beyond your project's budget.

Within this section, or under a separate heading, you might include a list of literature material that you will need to perform your project – for example, specific journals, company reports, books etc. Once again, if these materials are unavailable then realistically your project may be unsuitable and you may need to change its focus or direction. Access to particular companies for performing case studies might also be identified here. Without this access your project might flounder so it is important to show that you have contacts that can be utilised.

11. Project plan. It is very useful to present a project plan as part of your proposal. This emphasises that the project is 'doable' in the time allowed, it shows that you have some idea of the work involved, and you have a clear pathway to follow in order to complete that work. The best way to present a project plan is by using a visual representation such as a *Gantt chart*. These figures are described in the next chapter but it is worth emphasising here that presentation of these charts is important and you should limit them to a single page. Spreading these plans over several pages makes them difficult to read, and for a proposal a general overview is all that is required.

2.3.4 *Reviewing your proposal*

The second golden rule for preparing a project proposal states that you should proofread your complete proposal thoroughly.

You should check your proposal for spelling mistakes, omissions and grammatical errors. Have you included all the sections you were supposed to and

34   CHOOSING A PROJECT AND WRITING A PROPOSAL

have you completed those sections in sufficient depth? Is the proposal well presented (typed rather than handwritten, for example)? Do the sections flow logically together?

The following are two examples of undergraduate, final year information systems project proposals. Both proposals represent the same project and have been kept short for clarity.

Title:
   Software migration.
Project type:

Aims and objectives:
   Migrate a series of software applications from a mainframe to a client/server systam within a local company.
Outcomes and deliverables:
   - Connectivity to the mainframe for approx 1000 PCs;
   - Full integration into a client server environment;
   - Education of users;
   - Coding and testing complted.
Research methodology:
   PRINCE.
Hardware and software requirements:
   All available at local compnay.

This proposal is quite poor. Its *Title* is rather vague and only represents the type of project that is being proposed. The section identifying *Project type* has been left blank and the *Aims and objectives* represent a basic, technical, industry-type project with no academic content or justification. Expected *Outcomes and deliverables* emphasise this point and merely identify the technical outcomes of the project. The *Research methodology* section identifies the method that will be evaluated, rather than the research methods that will be employed. The proposal also includes a number of spelling mistakes and abbreviations. Overall, although this project may be acceptable within industry, it lacks any academic quality or rigour and is poorly presented.

Let's look at this project proposal from a new angle:

Title:
   Project management issues of software migration.
Project type:
   Evaluation project, industry based.

Aims and objectives:
Aim: To evaluate the use of the PRINCE method as a means to manage the migration of software from a mainframe to a client/server system.
Objectives: An evaluation of tools and methods to assist the technical aspects of the migration and organisational management aspects.
Evaluation of similar companies performing migration for comparative purposes.
The migration of a series of applications at a local company (to which access has been obtained) will be used as a vehicle for critically evaluating the PRINCE method in particular.
Outcomes and deliverables:
A report detailing the following:
- an explanation of the perceived benefits of such a migration;
- an analysis of the difficulties experienced;
- a critical evaluation of the PRINCE methodology and its application;
- an outline methodology for future migration projects;
- a discussion and evaluation of alternative tools and methods for software migration.

Research methodology:
Case study, action research.
Hardware and software requirements:
All available at a local company.

This proposal is a far better representation of an academic project than the first. Although the project is based on the same software migration, it identifies, far more clearly, the academic side of the project and the critical evaluation required by such projects. All sections are now completed correctly; for example, *Research methodology* identifies those methods actually employed and *Project type* has now been identified. The proposal reads well and has been checked for errors and omissions.

2.4 Choosing your supervisor

If you are lucky enough to be able to choose your own project supervisor there are a number of considerations you should contemplate when making your choice. Sharp and Howard (1996: 28–29) identify five questions that students should ask of potential supervisors:

1. What are their records in terms of student completions?
2. What are their views on the management of student research – and, in particular, the supervisor's role in it?

3. How eminent are they in their specialisms?
4. In addition to being knowledgeable about their subjects have they high competence in research methodology?
5. How accessible are they likely to be?

The fifth point noted here can relate not only to a supervisor's general availability, but to their approachability as well. It is all very well being able to see your supervisor regularly, but if you do not trust them, or get along with them, this time is wasted.

Supervisors come in various shapes and sizes but, to emphasise, the main points you should be looking for are accessibility (in terms of availability and approachability) and expertise (in terms of the subject area *and* supervisory skills). Chapter 5 looks in more detail at the student/supervisor relationship and discusses how to manage the time you spend with your supervisor effectively.

2.5 Summary

- Choosing the right project is probably the most important stage of any project.
- A number of techniques have been presented that you can use to assist you with choosing a suitable project.
- When preparing a proposal there are two golden rules: follow any guidelines precisely and proofread it thoroughly.
- A project proposal should include, at least implicitly, background, related research, identification of a gap, and how your project fills that gap.
- Project proposals should include, at the very least, the following sections: project title, aims and objectives, and expected outcomes/deliverables.
- Questions have been presented that you should ask yourself before you choose your project supervisor – if this is possible within your own institution.

2.6 Exercises

1. Try to build an RTM, relevance tree and/or spider diagram for your own computing project.
2. Can you improve the project proposal presented in Section 2.3.4.?
3. Put together a proposal for your own project using ideas and skills you have learnt.

CHAPTER 3
Project planning

Aims
To introduce the basics of project planning.

Learning objectives
When you have completed this chapter, you should be able to:

- describe the typical stages of an academic computing project;
- define a project in terms of aims and objectives;
- discuss the activities performed during the initial planning stage of a project;
- understand the use of project management techniques for project planning.

3.1 Introduction

All projects progress through five main stages during their lifetime, from the time the project is established as an initial idea, to the time the project is finally completed. These stages apply to all kinds of projects, from your own academic computing project to large industrial projects spanning several years. At this level of detail specific activities that might be unique within academic computing projects are not of interest. At this level interest lies in the broader stages in which project activities are performed. Each of these stages requires managing in one way or another and there are different considerations you will have to make as your project progresses through these stages. The five main stages are:

1. Definition
2. Planning
3. Initiation
4. Control
5. Closure

Project definition and *project planning* collectively relate to your project's *inauguration*. Project inauguration refers to the activities you perform before you actually start work on the main body of the project itself. Project definition is the preliminary stage of this process and includes the activities presented in Chapter 2: deciding on your project and getting it approved by submitting an acceptable proposal. In addition, this stage also includes establishing a more detailed project definition in order to prepare the ground for project planning. Project planning is the stage in which you decide how you will fulfil your aims by identifying and deciding on how to approach the work you need to perform. Project definition and project planning are the focus of this chapter.

The following three stages of the process represent the main 'bulk' of your project work – that is, actually 'doing' your project and working on developing the project's product. The project's product in this context represents a product in the widest sense of the term. Your project's product would be your written report, a fully documented piece of software, a new model or algorithm, a literature survey, a case study and so on. The product represents your project's expected outcome and deliverable.

Initiation represents the activities that you perform to start the main content of your project. It involves arranging yourself into some kind of routine and can include the initial definitive work you perform on your literature survey. If you are working on a group project you will have to assign tasks to, and organise, other members of your project team. You will arrange to meet with your project supervisor and lay down some ground rules and routines for the work ahead.

Once you have organised yourself, and your project is under way, you will need to *control* it as it is progressing. Project control is covered in detail in Chapter 5. The last stage of any project is *closure*. In your computing project this will represent the final completion of your project, writing up your report, perhaps preparing for a final presentation or viva voce examination, completing any programs and associated documentation and finally handing everything in. How you complete your project by performing these activities is the subject of Chapters 6 and 7.

3.2 Project definition

The purpose of project definition is to clearly specify what it is you hope to achieve with your project. As mentioned above, this stage initially includes deciding on your project and putting together a proposal (covered in Chapter 2). In many ways your project definition and your initial project proposal are closely linked. They should both be written at the start of your project. While your proposal aims to get your project accepted, your definition will help to clarify what it is you are really setting out to achieve.

Your project definition must identify the *aims* and *objectives* of your intended work. Chapter 2 briefly introduced the difference between aims and objectives for the purposes of producing a project proposal. In this section these ideas are extended so that your project can be defined clearly in these terms. Defining your project in this way is important for a number of reasons:

- If you have difficulty defining your project in terms of aims and objectives then you will have difficulty deciding on the work you ought to be doing and what your focus will be. It might also mean that your understanding of the subject area is lacking and you need to do some additional preliminary research in the topic area or, more drastically, choose an alternative project.
- It gives you a clear target at which to aim. This provides a continual reference point against which you can assess your progress.
- It provides you with a means of evaluating your success at the end. For example, did you achieve all that you intended to do or more?

3.2.1 Defining your aims

Your project should be defined at two levels. At the top level you define your project's aim or *goal*. All projects have one major aim that they hope to achieve and your computing project is no exception. If you are ever in any doubt over what work you ought to be doing or which direction you ought to be taking, you can refer to your project's aim to guide you. Examples of typical aims for computing projects are:

- To evaluate the effectiveness of requirements capture techniques in small software development companies in the UK.
- To develop and evaluate a user interface for statistical software packages.
- To design a methodology for GUI development of technical courseware material.
- To produce an evaluation of fourth generation languages for database development.

Each of these aims provides you with an understanding of that project's main purpose. They identify the area of investigation and the focus of the intended work. In order to achieve these aims each project will have a set of *objectives*: smaller sub-goals that are significant steps towards achieving the project's aim.

3.2.2 Setting objectives

As Chapter 2 specified, objectives identify significant measurable achievements you hope to make that build towards the ultimate aim of your project. Having identified and defined your project's aim, you should continue to define your project in terms of its objectives. For a project expected to last approximately one year, you wouldn't expect to identify more than twelve objectives for your project. If your project has more objectives than this it may be that you are attempting to do too much or that you are breaking your project down into too much detail.

Take, as an example, a computing project that is going to evaluate artificial neural networks for predicting stock market indices (not an easy task!). You might identify the following aims and objectives for this project:

Project's aim:

- To develop and evaluate an artificial neural network to predict stock market indices.

Project's objectives:

1. Complete literature search and literature review of existing stock market prediction techniques;
2. Develop a suitable artificial neural network model;
3. Identify and collect suitable data for analyses and evaluation;
4. Evaluate the model using appropriate statistical techniques;
5. Complete final report.

Note how the objectives build towards the ultimate aim of the project. They also appear in approximately chronological order – in other words, they identify the order in which you would expect to tackle the work. Notice, also, how you could further break down these objectives. For example, objective 2 would need you to investigate, evaluate and identify a suitable tool and topology before you could develop a suitable neural network. Objective 4 may require you to investigate and learn how to use some suitable statistical techniques or statistical software packages. However, breaking objectives down into lower and lower levels of detail serves little purpose other than to cloud your vision of your ultimate goal. This will become clear in the following section, which discusses how to break down the actual work you will need to do to complete your project using *work breakdown structures*.

3.3 Project planning

Although you are now clear about what you intend to achieve with your project, what you now need to identify is the work you need to do in order to fulfil these aims. Project planning assists you by identifying the work you need to perform, clarifying the order in which you should tackle the work, and revealing how long you need to do it. It is at this point that you may realise that your project is either overly complex or of insufficient depth for the

PROJECT PLANNING 41

requirements of your course. You may then decide to redefine your project (expanding or reducing its scope) before replanning your work once more.

Project planning is performed through a series of six steps that utilise a number of project management techniques:

- Work breakdown
- Time estimates
- Milestone identification
- Activity sequencing
- Scheduling
- Replanning

Three techniques that are suitable are *work breakdown structures*, *activity networks* and *Gantt charts*. Each of these techniques will be looked at in turn as the six steps of project planning are discussed.

3.3.1 **Step 1: Work breakdown**

Work breakdown structures (WBSs) are used to break your project down into lower and lower levels of detail to reveal exactly what work you will need to do to complete your project. You should begin a WBS by breaking your project down into its main objectives that you identified during your project's definition. You might only be able to break your project down into two or three main areas of work or you might be able to identify several broad areas of activity.

Figure 3.1 provides an example of a WBS for the artificial neural network

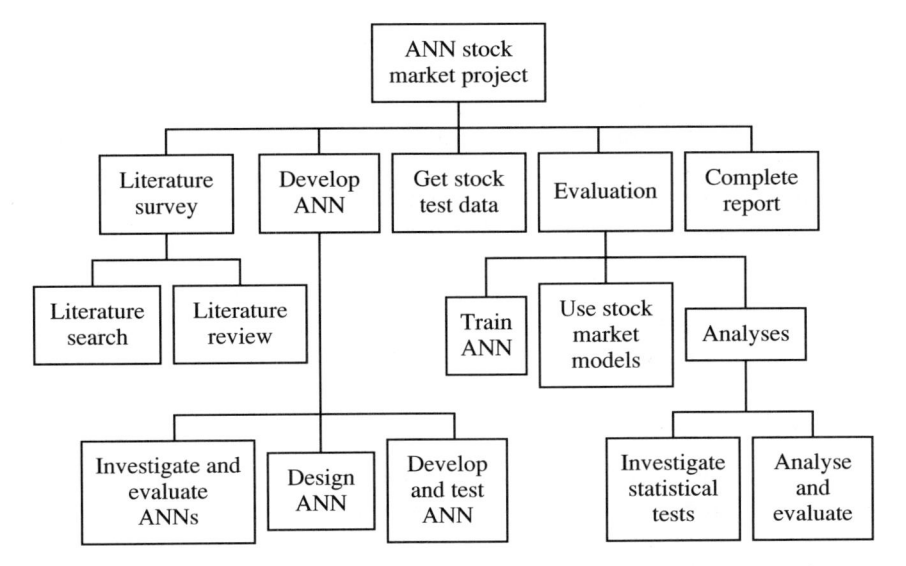

Figure 3.1 *An example of a work breakdown structure*

(ANN) stock market project introduced earlier. Five main objectives have been identified that need to be performed to complete this project. Notice how these tasks represent the five objectives identified earlier.

You should continue to develop your WBS by breaking your objectives down into lower and lower levels of detail. You may well find that some activities can be broken down further than others. For example, in Figure 3.1, it has been identified in the WBS that the *Literature survey* will actually require the completion of a *Literature search* and a *Literature review* (although in Chapter 4 you will see that the literature survey process is much more complicated than this). Developing the ANN will first involve investigating and evaluating ANN topologies and tools (*Investigate and evaluate ANNs*) before designing the ANN (*Design ANN*) and then developing and testing it (*Develop and test ANN*).

Evaluation will involve three activities: training the ANN (*Train ANN*), using the market models evaluated from the literature review (*Use stock market models*) and performing *Analyses* of the two approaches. Notice how *Analyses* has been broken down into another level of detail, showing that it requires an investigation and application of appropriate statistical tests and tools (*Investigate statistical tests*) before analysing and evaluating the results (*Analyse and evaluate*).

As you break down your project in this way you should ensure that tasks at all levels are separate from one another and an activity in one part of the structure is not repeated or revealed within another area of work. If this happens you may be duplicating effort on your project unnecessarily or your WBS may be incorrect.

You can continue to break these activities down further but you must stop somewhere otherwise you could be identifying work that might take five minutes to complete! A general rule of thumb is that you should continue to break your project down into activities that take no less than around 5% of your project's total duration. For example, there is little point in identifying activities that will take you less than a week to complete in a six-month project. If you do this you may spend more time adjusting and controlling your plans as your project progresses than actually doing any work. There are always unforeseen events in projects, and activities will invariably take longer than you expect. Planning at too fine a detail is unwise as things will certainly happen to affect minutely planned activities before your project has finished.

3.3.2 Step 2: Time estimates

Identifying a project's aims and objectives provides little indication of exactly how long the project will take to complete. You would hope that your project is of a suitable scope to keep you busy during the allotted time and is of sufficient depth for you to obtain a good grade. However, it is not until you break the project down using a WBS that you can really begin to see just how much work is involved.

Now that the project is broken down into a number of tasks it is much easier to estimate how long the project will take. It is far harder, for example, to predict how long it will take to complete the project's *Evaluation* than it is to predict the effort needed for individual tasks that make up that activity: *Train a neural network*, *Use stock market models* and perform the *Analyses*. You may, however, feel that these lower-level tasks are still not explicit enough, and there is nothing to stop you breaking them down further within reason. This is just what was done with the *Analyses* activity in the example project.

Focusing now on the lowest level of the WBS, it is possible to make reasonably accurate predictions of the effort needed to perform these activities and consequently the project as a whole. For example, using the WBS in Figure 3.1, the time estimates in Table 3.1 can be made for the *lowest* level tasks.

You should be reasonably happy with this estimate of the total project effort as it is much more accurate than you could have achieved working from the project's title alone. You might now realise that, perhaps, you have aimed to do too much in the time available and need to reduce what you intend to achieve. Alternatively you might decide to allocate yourself less time to complete particular activities if you feel your estimates for these tasks were conservative.

3.3.3 **Step 3: Milestone identification**

Milestones are significant steps towards the completion of a project. They help you to appreciate your progress by providing you with intermediate reference points. This enables you to assess, at the earliest opportunity, how you are progressing against your planned schedule. Because you know these milestones

Table 3.1 *Time estimates for example project*

Activity	Estimated duration
Literature search	8 weeks
Literature review	4 weeks
Investigate and evaluate ANNs	4 weeks
Design ANN	4 weeks
Develop and test ANN	2 weeks
Get stock test data	1 week
Train ANN	1 week
Use stock market models	2 weeks
Investigate statistical tests	2 weeks
Analyse and evaluate	4 weeks
Complete report	8 weeks
Total effort	40 weeks (approximately 10 months)

are leading you towards the ultimate goal of your project you can use them as intermediate goals at which to aim. Figure 3.2 provides a simple illustration of this point. In this figure the milestones are providing mini targets that you can use to focus your work in the short term.

To identify milestones you should focus on your project's work breakdown structure and identify any key stages that appear to be significant breakthroughs in your project's progress. It is best to do this at the top level of the WBS and use some (if not all) of your project's objectives as milestones. These milestones then identify areas of work that, when completed, indicate you have achieved a significant step along the way. The number of milestones that you will identify for your project will vary depending on the project's size. For a year-long project, six or seven milestones should be more than adequate as these would represent, on average, the completion of approximately two months' work. One milestone you will always identify is the project's completion.

For simplicity only two milestones will be identified in the example project, the completion of the literature survey (milestone 1; M1) and the completion of the project as a whole (milestone 2; M2). M1 shows that a significant step has been made in completing the project's foundation. You would expect to achieve this milestone within the first 12 weeks. M2 is the end of the project and clearly represents a significant event in the work! How these milestones are symbolised in the project plan is discussed in the following sections.

3.3.4 Step 4: Activity sequencing

You now have an understanding of the work you need to perform in the project and the effort required to complete the individual tasks involved. An *activity network* can now be used to identify the order in which you should perform that work. Activity networks were first developed towards the end of the 1950s and are sometimes referred to as PERT networks, CPM or network diagrams. We will look at the simplest form of these diagrams, in which activities are represented by rectangles or *nodes* (known as activity-on-the-node).

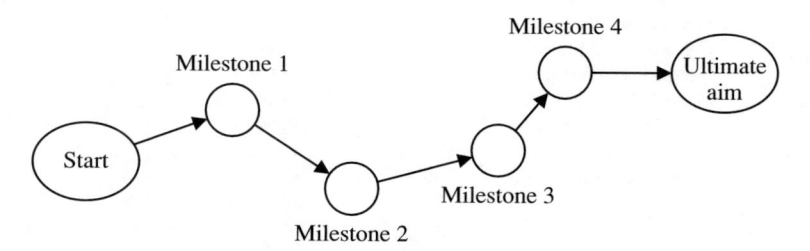

Figure 3.2 *Milestones leading to the project's ultimate aim*

Activity-on-the-node diagrams represent the tasks you are performing in your project as nodes connected by arrows. The arrows show the order in which activities must be performed.

For example, in Figure 3.3, Task A can start at any time as it does not rely on any other task completing. Task A would therefore start at the beginning of the project. Task B cannot start until Task A has finished and Task D can only start after *both* tasks B and C have completed successfully. Task C is similar to Task B in that it cannot start until Task A has ended.

If this representation is applied to the example stock market project introduced earlier it results in the activity-on-the-node representation shown in Figure 3.4. In this example the completion of the project's report has been identified as an activity that is performed during the last eight weeks of the project. In reality, however, you would probably be working on your project's report throughout the lifetime of your project and the activity identified here really represents the final drawing together of the report: checking and completing your references, writing your abstract and contents listing, proofreading and spell checking.

There are three additions to Figure 3.4 that are not shown in Figure 3.3 and which have yet to be explained. The first point to note is that the milestones identified earlier have been included as ovals called M1 and M2, M1 being the completed literature survey and M2 representing the completed project. Notice how these have been placed in the relevant positions on the diagram and represent the completion of the significant step they are identifying.

The second point to note is that dates and figures have been added to each task node. Each activity now has two figures: the start date of the activity, shown at the top left of each node, and the duration of the activity (in weeks) shown on the top right. These durations are taken from the time estimates made earlier in Table 3.1. It is up to you what time 'granularity' you use for your project (hours, days, weeks, months or even years) but in a project of this size weeks or months are suitable.

For simplicity it will be assumed that a month consists of exactly four weeks and there are no breaks in the project for holidays! However, in reality holidays, sickness, revision, field trips and so on can often impede your progress, and these events should be considered when forming project plans.

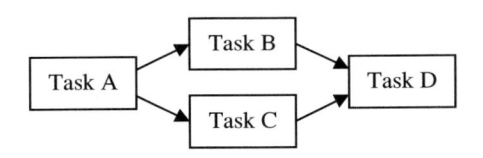

Figure 3.3 *An example of a simple activity-on-the-node diagram*

46 PROJECT PLANNING

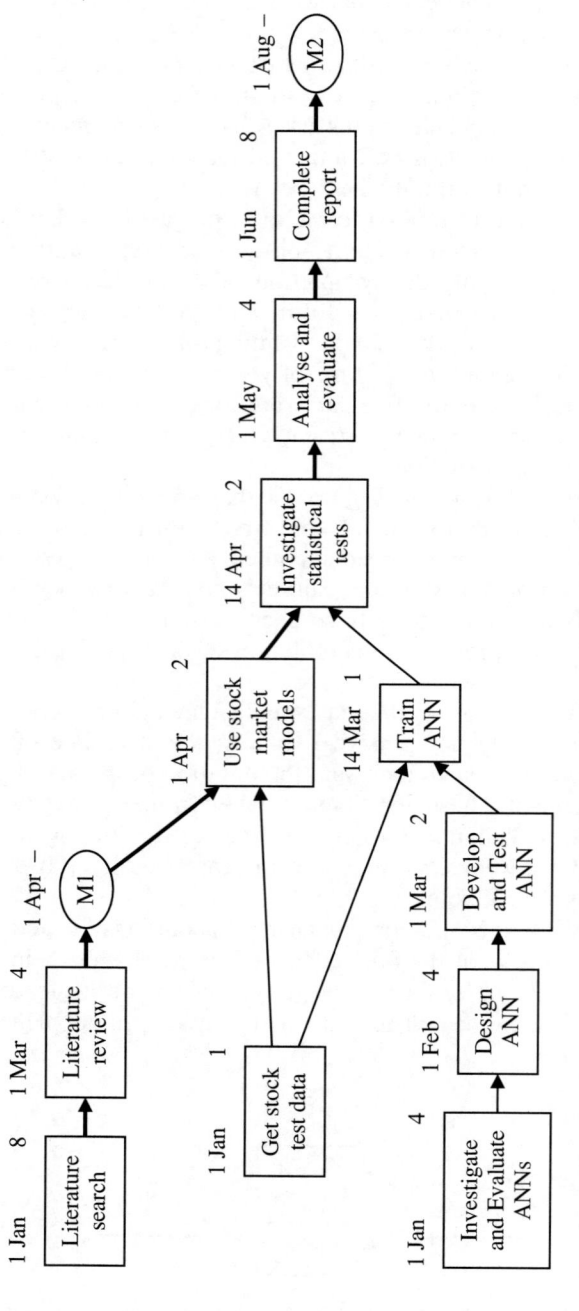

Figure 3.4 An example of an activity network

The date, which is noted at the top left-hand corner of each activity, represents the time at which that activity will start. For activities that can start straight away (i.e. they do not need any other activities to have completed beforehand) this is simply the start date of the project. In the example, three activities can start straight away – *Literature search*, *Get stock test data* and *Investigate and evaluate ANNs*. All these activities have the same start time, 1 January, which represents the start date of the project overall.

To calculate the start times of subsequent activities it is necessary to look at the tasks leading to them. For example, in this simple case, the *Literature review* can begin as soon as the *Literature search* has completed. As the *Literature search* takes eight weeks to complete (approximately two months) the *Literature review* can begin from 1 March onwards. The first milestone (M1, complete literature survey) occurs when this review is completed and consequently, as the review takes four weeks to complete (approximately one month), M1 will occur on 1 April. Notice also how M1 has no duration assigned to it because it does not represent any work as such but an event in time.

Calculating the start time for activities with more than one task leading into them is not quite so straightforward. When two or more tasks lead into another, that task can only start when *all* preceding tasks have completed. For example, in Figure 3.4 notice that *Train ANN* starts on 14 March – this is when you would expect *Develop and test ANN* to complete, *not* when *Get stock test data* has completed. Remember that subsequent activities can only begin when *all* preceding activities leading to them have completed.

Continuing with the calculation of start times for each activity in the project, the final milestone, M2 (completed project), is reached. Thus it is possible to conclude that the project should be completed by 1 August. However, this may be optimistic as it does not account for any delays or problems that might occur.

The final addition to this network diagram is the *critical path*, which still requires explanation. This path is the longest route through the project network and is represented in Figure 3.4 by the bolder arrowed lines. It shows the activities in the project that must not be delayed, as to do so will delay the project overall. For example, if *Complete report* were to take twelve weeks instead of eight, the project would now finish on 1 September – four weeks later than before. This is because *Complete report* lies on the critical path and any delay to this activity will affect the project overall.

To identify the critical path you work backwards through the network diagram. Begin, therefore, at M2 and look to see which task(s) leading to this milestone is causing it to occur on 1 August. There is only one activity in this case leading into M2, *Complete report*, so this task is on the critical path. Looking next at *Complete report* see, once again, that only one task leads into it – *Analyse and evaluate*. Consequently, *Analyse and evaluate* must also be on the critical path.

You continue to work your way backwards through the network until you either reach the project's start or an activity that has two or more activities leading into it. In the latter case *Investigate statistical tests* is the first activity in this situation. However, just as before, you look back through the network to see which activity is forcing *Investigate statistical tests* to start on 14 April and see that, in this case, it is *Use stock market models*, not *Train ANN*. *Use stock market models* is also, therefore, on the critical path. Continue in this way, working backwards through the network, until you reach the start of the project – in this case ending up at the *Literature search*. The critical path is thus identified by the bolder arrowed lines linking each of these critical activities together.

There is no reason why you cannot have more than one critical path in your project network. In some cases two or more activities may force a following task to start on a particular date. In these cases, proceed as before, following all critical paths back to the start of the project or to a point where they rejoin. The activity network is now complete.

This representation has made two assumptions. The first is that you can perform several tasks simultaneously. This often happens in computing projects where you might, for example, be performing aspects of your literature survey alongside an initial systems analysis or program design. This also allows you to avoid becoming bored with one activity or another because you can switch between them as your project progresses. However, although identifying several simultaneous tasks may be satisfactory for group projects, where several members of the project team can work on tasks separately, for individual projects this can cause a problem. To identify instances when you are expecting yourself to work on too many activities simultaneously, and to see how you can deal with this problem, you must use a *Gantt chart*, which is introduced in the following section.

The second assumption made is that once activities are completed they are finished with and your project moves on. In reality, however, activities exist that are ongoing throughout the lifetime of your project; for example, the literature survey and report writing activities. However, emphasis on these changes as the project progresses. There are also situations where activities are repeated and you find yourself performing a loop – for example, the literature search and literature review, which are part of the repetitive literature survey process discussed in Chapter 4. A particular example of loops occurring within software development projects is when an evolutionary delivery approach is being used.

These situations cannot be planned explicitly using ordinary activity network diagrams, and although there are some networking techniques that can be used to identify repetition and loops, they are not widely available. Consequently, project planning tends to identify distinct activities that occur either in parallel or in sequence and limits activity network plans to these representations.

3.3.5 Step 5: Scheduling

Gantt charts are similar to activity networks in that they attempt to represent a project in diagrammatical form. However, unlike activity networks, which show the relationships between tasks, Gantt charts show explicitly the durations of activities and identify instances when tasks are performed simultaneously.

Just like activity networks, Gantt charts represent a project's activities as nodes. In this case, however, the length of each node is used to signify the duration of each activity. For example, in Figure 3.5 a Gantt chart is presented for the example project. The scale running along the bottom of this chart represents the dates during which the project is performed. Notice how each activity in this chart is represented by a rectangle which is as long as each activity's estimated duration. For example, the *Literature search* lasts for two months starting at the beginning of the project. It is therefore drawn up until 1 March. The *Literature review* follows on from the *Literature search* and lasts for one month – again shown by the length of the task box.

It is important to keep an eye on the activity network when drawing a Gantt chart to ensure that activities are performed in the correct sequence and that

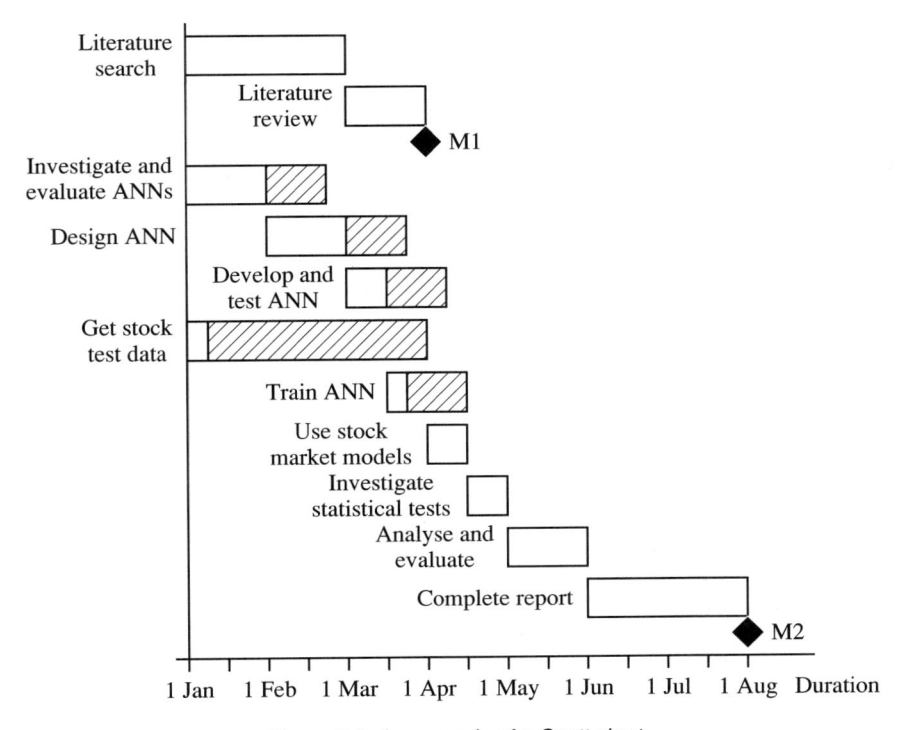

Figure 3.5 *An example of a Gantt chart*

activities do not start in the Gantt chart before all their preceding tasks have completed. Some Gantt charts allow you to include the arrowed lines linking activities like those in the activity network. However, trying to include all this information on one diagram does lead to the diagram becoming very messy and difficult to follow.

The Gantt chart also differs from the activity network in that milestones are now represented by diamonds. In addition, notice how activities that do not fall on the critical path of the activity network have shaded extensions to them. These shaded areas represent an activity's *slack* or *float* time. Remember that activities on the critical path cannot be delayed without delaying the project overall. This means that activities that do not lie on the critical path can be delayed to some extent without affecting the project. The extent to which an activity can be delayed without affecting the project is called its slack or float time.

To identify slack time you need to focus on activities that do not lie on the critical path. You then work your way backwards through your project until you meet one of these activities. In the example, looking at the activity network in Figure 3.4, the first activity encountered, working back through the network, that does not lie on the critical path is *Train ANN*. *Train ANN* leads into *Investigate statistical tests*, which is on the critical path. As long as *Train ANN* is not delayed for so long that it starts to delay *Investigate statistical tests* the project will not be affected. Thus, *Train ANN* could be delayed so that it finishes no later than the start of *Investigate statistical tests*. This delay represents the slack time of *Train ANN* and is shown as a shaded area in Figure 3.5.

Because *Investigate and evaluate ANNs*, *Design ANNs* and *Develop and test ANN* all lead into *Train ANN*, these activities may also be delayed by the same duration as *Train ANN* without affecting the project. Consequently, these activities have the same float applied to them as *Train ANN* (i.e. three weeks). *Get stock test data* is the only other activity not lying on the critical path that still needs considering. This activity must complete before *Use stock market models* can begin. Thus, *Get stock test data* can be delayed up until 1 April but notice that it would delay *Train ANN* by two weeks if it were. This is acceptable because *Train ANN* is not on the critical path and thus delaying it by two weeks will not impact on the project. The Gantt chart is now complete.

What this chart now highlights is that there are times when you need to perform more than one activity at a time. For example, looking at the first week of the project in January, you will see how you should be working on the *Literature search*, *Investigate ANNs* and *Get stock test data* all at the same time. For group projects this is not a problem as these tasks can be assigned between team members. However, for individual projects, this might well be unacceptable and something needs to be done about it.

One solution might be to use the float time on various activities. For example, *Get stock test data* could be delayed for a few weeks without affecting the project overall and it would reduce the number of activities that needed to be performed during the first week of the project. However, this is only putting off the inevitable. At some stage in the project *Get stock test data* will have to be done and it will inevitably clash with some other work then. The problem lies in the fact that ten months' worth of work is being attempted within seven months with only one person available. This is impossible, unless you are able to do more than one activity at a time. If you cannot, then you must accept that your project will take ten months to complete and you should adjust your Gantt chart accordingly.

Project management software packages are well suited to these kinds of problems – known as *scheduling*. They attempt to balance out people's time on projects in order to achieve a satisfactory allocation of work over a project's life span.

In this case, a popular project management package called Microsoft Project has been used. Figure 3.6 shows a print-out of a Gantt chart from this package for the example project. Notice how similar this is to the representation shown in Figure 3.5. Microsoft Project was then used to replan the project on the understanding that only one person was available to do the work. Microsoft Project rescheduled the plan to that shown in Figure 3.7. Notice how the project is now scheduled to last for ten months, finishing at the end of October, and only one activity is being performed at any one time. However, this is not necessarily an ideal solution as, for example, there now appears to be quite a delay between performing the *Literature search* and writing the *Literature review* – two activities that, in reality, are closely intertwined. With this in mind, you should always pay close attention to scheduling adjustments that are made by project management software tools.

3.3.6 **Step 6: Replanning**

Now that you have completed all your plans you may realise that you are trying to do too much in the time available. Replanning simply means that you go back through your plans, adjusting and rescheduling them accordingly. Project management software tools are particularly useful for making these changes and assessing the impact of your adjustments. However, try not to spend too long on this stage by getting drawn into the usability of these tools and end up using them for their own sake. You may find yourself replanning and rescheduling at minute levels of detail rather than getting on with the real work of your project.

Note, also, that plans you have produced should not be cast in stone. For instance, in the example project you may find that after completing your investigation of ANNs you decide that it might be more appropriate to use an off-the-shelf package rather than develop your own ANN model. This will clearly lead to some reworking of the plan and may release some time to concentrate on other activities.

52 PROJECT PLANNING

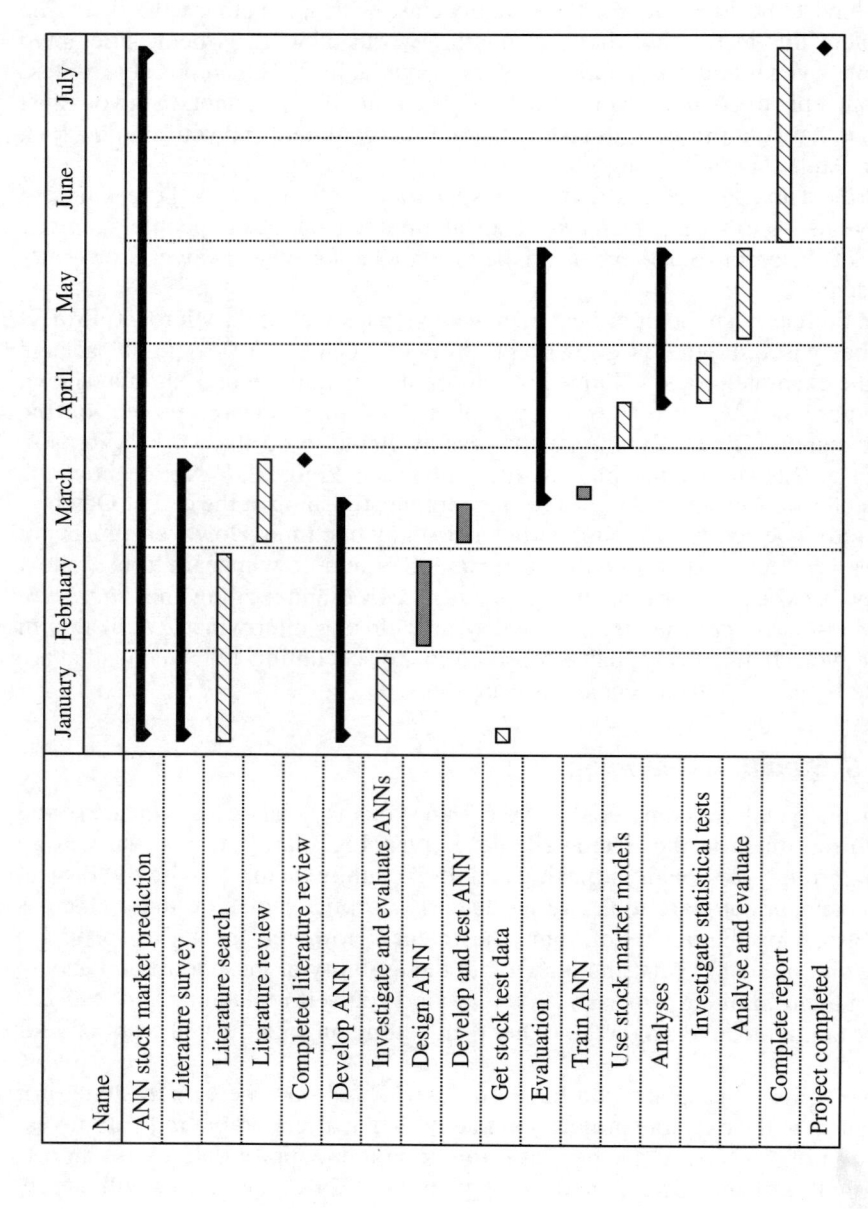

Figure 3.6 *Microsoft Project's Gantt chart of example project*

PROJECT PLANNING 53

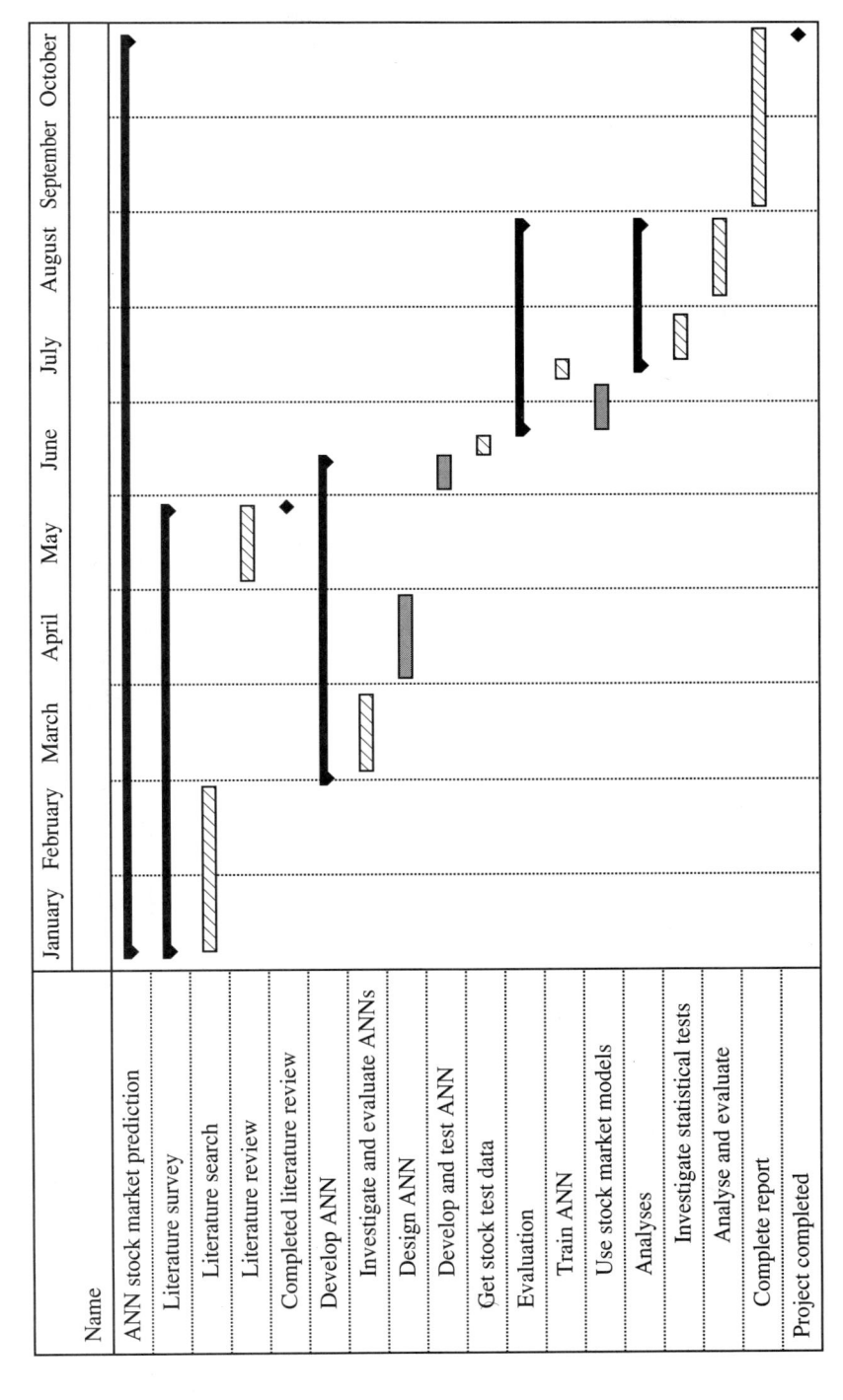

Figure 3.7 *Scheduled Gantt chart of example project*

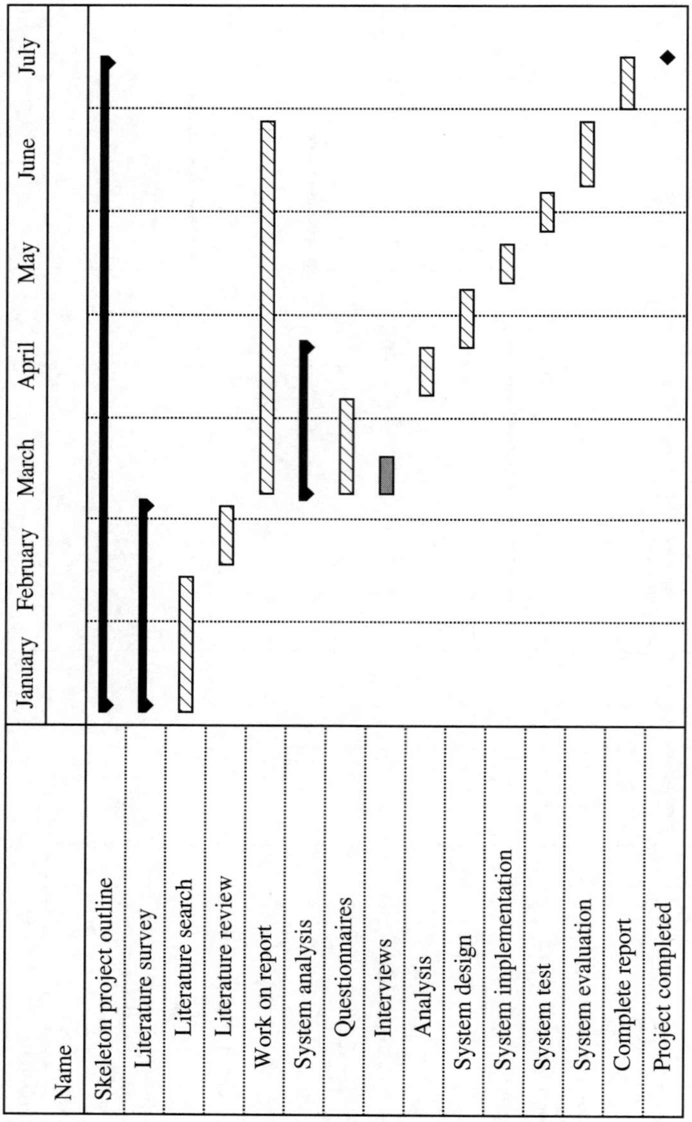

54 PROJECT PLANNING

Figure 3.8 Example rolling wave skeleton plan for a system development project

3.3.7 **Rolling wave planning**

A technique that can help you when your project is not all that clear is *rolling wave planning*. Rolling wave planning means that you do not construct a detailed project plan at the project's inception but a 'skeleton' plan which identifies the key stages of your project. Your project planning is thus performed 'on the fly' as your project progresses. You make decisions as to where you are actually heading and what work you will have to perform in the following stage of your project as you complete previous stages. Thus, your planning detail ebbs and flows (like a rolling wave) as your project progresses and you make decisions on where to go and what to do next.

As a skeleton plan is relatively broad it can be suitable for many projects. Although it is of little use if you don't have *any* idea of what you want to do, it can help you to identify universal milestones that you must adhere to – for example, complete a literature survey, hand in your final report and so on – whatever these turn out to be. Figure 3.8 provides an example of a typical rolling wave, skeleton plan – in this case a system development-type project that lasts for about six months. Although this plan does not provide explicit detail about what this project is really about, it does identify the significant tasks that need to be completed and by when.

3.4 **Summary**

- Project planning consists of two stages: defining what it is you want to achieve and planning how you will achieve this. Project definition involves identifying your project's aims and objectives.
- Planning itself consists of six steps: identifying the tasks involved using *work breakdown structures*, estimating the duration of these tasks, identifying critical stages in your project called *milestones*, identifying the order in which activities should be performed using *activity networks*, scheduling your time using *Gantt charts* so that you are not trying to do more than you can physically achieve, and replanning your project to fit the time available.
- Project management software packages, such as Microsoft Project, can be used to assist you with planning and managing your project. While you can put together your own Gantt charts and activity networks by hand, such as those shown in Figures 3.4 and 3.5, project management software tools can automate this process for you. However, these packages do take time to learn and you can often find yourself spending more time planning and tweaking your project with these packages than actually doing any real work.

3.5 Further reading

Burton, C. and Michael, N. (1992) *A Practical Guide to Project Management*, Kogan Page, London.

Weiss, J.W. and Wysocki, R.K. (1992) *5-Phase Project Management, A Practical Planning and Implementation Guide*, Addison-Wesley, Reading, Massachusetts.

3.6 Exercises

1. Try to identify objectives for the example projects mentioned in Section 3.2.1.
2. Identify aims and objectives for your own computing project.
3. Follow the six steps of planning to complete your project's plan.

PART II

Conducting your project

CHAPTER 4
Literature searching and literature reviews

Aims
To introduce the skills of literature surveys.

Learning objectives
When you have completed this chapter, you should be able to:

- understand the process of literature surveys;
- define and conduct a literature search;
- manage information obtained during a literature search;
- understand how to conduct critical evaluation;
- write a literature review.

4.1 Introduction

In virtually all computing projects (especially at postgraduate level) you are assessed on what you submit at the end of the day – be it a written report, a working program, a specification, detailed system designs, test plans or whatever. However, it is often the initial investigative work that you perform that can make the difference between a good project and a borderline fail, even for practically-based programming projects in which the development of a piece of software is the main component. The initial foundation for your project is a *literature survey*. This survey is composed of two main components: a *literature search* and a *literature review*. The literature search represents the mechanics of looking for, sorting, managing and digesting research material that is available. The literature review represents your written understanding, critical evaluation, conceptualisation and presentation of the material you have obtained. A skill related closely to both of these components is *referencing*. How to reference material correctly is discussed in Chapter 6.

A literature survey acts as an introduction to your computing project and serves a number of purposes:

- It justifies your project – that is, it shows that your project is worth

doing; the area that you are investigating is recognised and meaningful. At postgraduate level you will also be showing that your project is not merely repeating the work of others, but has a contribution to make, perhaps by identifying a current gap in the literature of your field of study which you intend to fill.
- It sets your project within context by discussing and critically evaluating past and current research in your area. Through this contextualisation you will identify how your project fits within, and contributes to, wider issues. This will depend on the level (postgraduate or undergraduate) of computing project you are undertaking.
- It provides other researchers with a starting point from which they can understand how your project evolved and to identify what literature is relevant to your project in order that they can continue where you left off.

Justification

The importance of a literature survey within academic projects cannot be overemphasised. For example, Figure 4.1 helps to illustrate a literature survey's contribution within the context of a computing project by analogy to building a block of flats. Although people might come from far and wide to visit your luxury penthouse on the top floor (i.e. they are interested in reading your *project report*), this penthouse (report) will be unstable, of poor quality and limited in its academic worth, if it doesn't rest on firm foundations (the literature survey). Sometimes students start their projects at the ground floor; tackling what they feel is the main content of their project without justifying it or identifying its context within the wider issues. This can often prove disastrous because the project is not properly planned, investigations are narrow, conclusions are weak, and impacts and influences of other relevant issues are ignored.

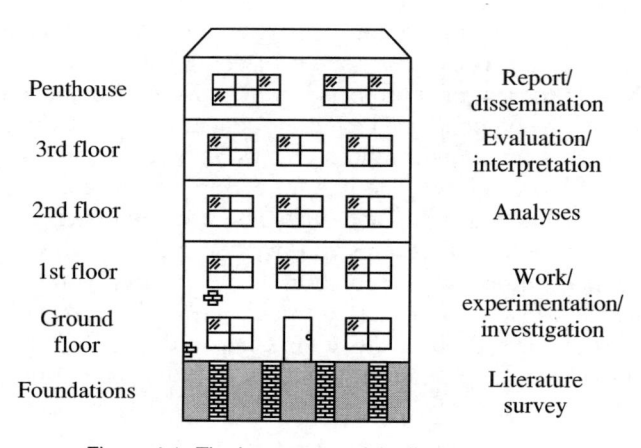

Figure 4.1 *The importance of the literature survey*

Context

It is very important for any academic project to justify its content by identifying how it fits into a broader context. Figure 4.2 shows two potential student projects; one at undergraduate level and one at postgraduate (PhD) level. This is an alternative viewpoint to that shown in Figure 1.1, which aimed to show your own understanding within world knowledge. Figure 4.2 represents a somewhat simplified interpretation of world thinking, knowledge, understanding, theories and philosophies (and an undergraduate project probably represents a lot less than the 10% of all world thinking as indicated in this diagram!). Advances to current understanding, through research discoveries and inventions, are shown as expansions to this domain by a dashed line. Conversely, contractions in world understanding might also occur as historical skills are forgotten. However, although Duell (Commissioner of the US Office of Patents) stated in 1899 that 'Everything that can be invented has been invented', on the whole, world knowledge continues to expand as new discoveries are made.

Figure 4.2 also recognises that the world is by no means at the limits of understanding and there are (possibly) an infinite number of discoveries and inventions yet to be made. This is highlighted by the isolated region towards the top right of the diagram. This knowledge domain may seem ridiculous and fanciful at the moment, based on current philosophies and understandings, but it might in future become an area of accepted theory and knowledge. For

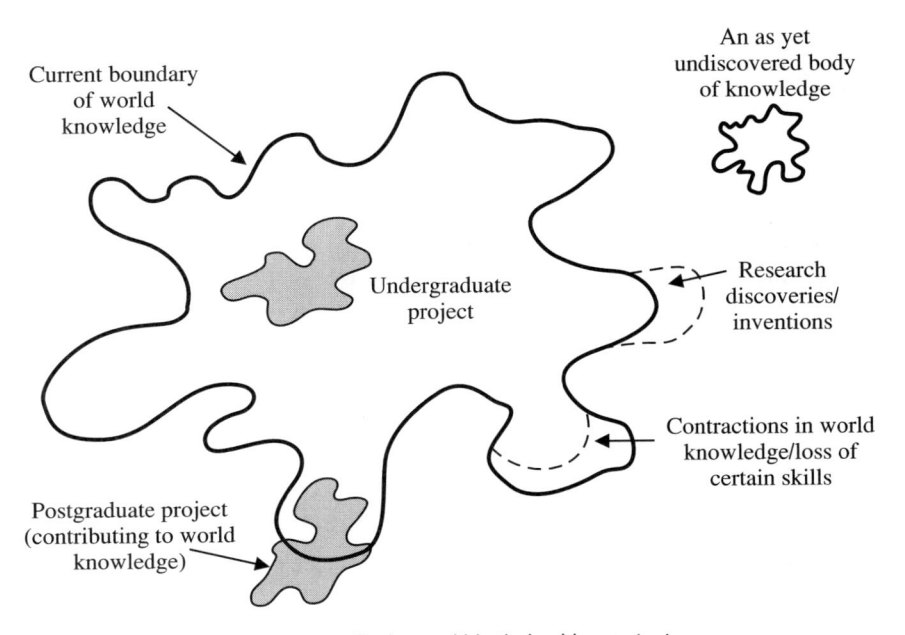

Figure 4.2 *Projects within their wider context*

example, 500 years ago people thought the earth was flat. The understanding that the earth was round and revolved around the sun appeared a ridiculous notion at that time and would have appeared as the disjoint region shown in Figure 4.2. World knowledge has now expanded to accept this understanding/belief within its boundaries. Other interesting examples where world understanding has changed over time are highlighted by the following two quotations:

> Computers of the future may weigh no more than 1.5 tons.
> *(Popular Mechanics* magazine, 1949)

> I think there is a world market for maybe five computers
> (Thomas Watson, IBM Chairman, 1943)

Postgraduate versus undergraduate projects

If you are pursuing a PhD, an MPhil or even an MSc your project should be at the boundaries of world understanding in your particular field of study – see Figure 4.2. Completing a PhD must enhance world knowledge. In other words, you would be expected to make a *contribution* to world knowledge and consequently expand its boundaries. An MPhil and an MSc, on the other hand, would not necessarily make a major contribution to knowledge, but they would be involved with an investigation into potential developments to world knowledge and be concerned with work at the boundaries.

At undergraduate level, however, this would not be expected. At this level you would be required to understand how your project fits into its wider context and have some appreciation of developments in that area. Examiners at undergraduate level are interested in your own ideas, interpretations, theories and concepts of the particular field of study. They are not expecting a major contribution to knowledge from your project at this level.

Figure 4.3 focuses more on the context of an individual undergraduate project. This figure shows how a project can draw on information from a number of different topic areas (in this case, two). This project's main focus is the overlap between these two subjects, although it does concentrate a little more on field B than field A. The project does not ignore issues from these two

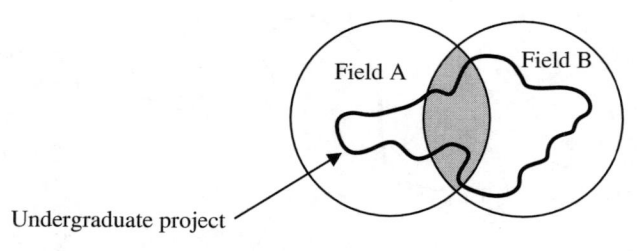

Figure 4.3 *An undergraduate project in context within two subject areas*

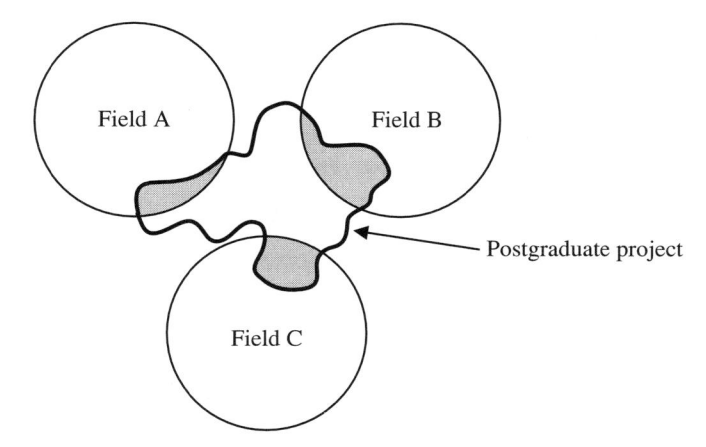

Figure 4.4 *A postgraduate project that draws together three previously unrelated subject areas*

fields on their own, but uses material from them to identify the broader context in which the project lies.

Figure 4.4 shows a potential PhD project along similar lines. This time the project might draw on three currently unrelated fields and contribute to knowledge by filling the gap between these fields. In both these cases the projects have been identified within their wider contexts and the reader has an understanding of how the projects draw together and focus on particular subject areas.

A starting point
Your literature survey also enables other people interested in your work to see the grounds from which your project developed. A thorough literature survey will give other researchers a starting point for their studies and provide anyone wishing to develop your project work further with a comprehensive literature base.

4.2 The literature survey process

In Chapter 3, when project planning was discussed, the literature survey was split into the two distinct, concurrent stages of the search and the review. For planning purposes it might well be acceptable to define the literature survey in this simplistic way to aid clarity. However, the literature survey process is more complicated than this. Although these two components represent the bulk of the work involved in performing a literature survey, there is more to a survey than just this. Figure 4.5 provides a far more accurate representation of

64 LITERATURE SEARCHING AND LITERATURE REVIEWS

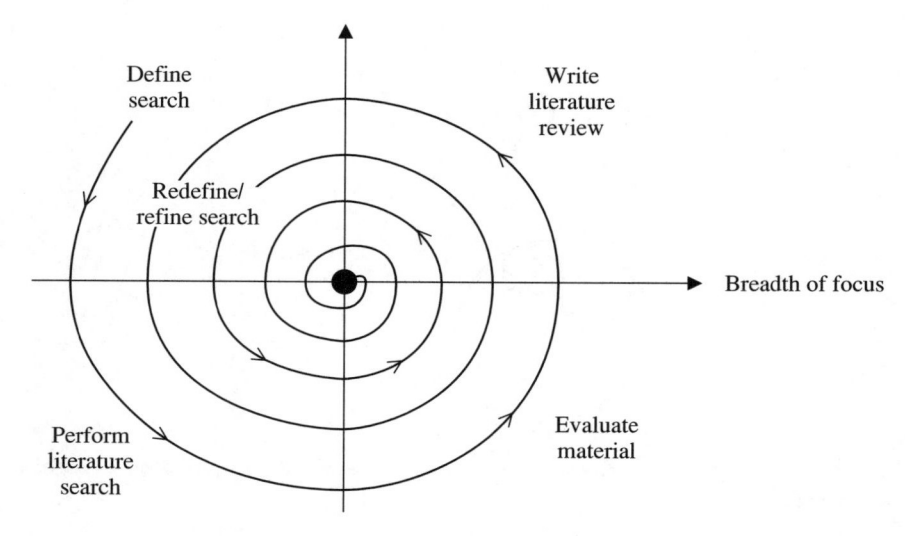

Figure 4.5 *The literature survey process*

this process. In this figure the angular axis represents time and the radial axis represents your subject focus.

The starting point for your literature survey is the *definition* of your literature search – starting in the top left-hand quadrant of Figure 4.5. This definition begins to identify the boundaries of your literature search, it identifies the topics in which you are interested and provides you with a starting point from which to focus on appropriate research material. This definition might be as simple as your subjective understanding of your project area and might lead you to popular texts in your field. You may, however, be more focused and limit your search definition to key authors, specific journals and/or particular research articles. Alternatively, you might want to use a conceptual model such as a *relevance tree*, *spider diagram* or *research territory map*, introduced in Chapter 2, whereby the relationships between topics within your project are identified. These conceptual maps will help you to identify the starting point for your literature search.

Continuing around the spiral of Figure 4.5, having decided broadly (or specifically) what you are interested in searching for, you can then begin to perform your *literature search* (this stage and the following two stages are discussed in more detail in separate sections later). Your literature search will provide you with material that requires your *critical evaluation*. This critical evaluation will provide you with a firm understanding of your chosen subject area and will form the basis of the next stage of the process – your *literature review*. Note that these stages are not independent – you will not visit your university's library, gather all the references you need, return to your desk, read and evaluate them and complete your literature review. You will perform some of these tasks in parallel. For example, you may be evaluating some articles while you wait for others on order through inter-library loans. You might read part of an article or a book relating to a topic you are currently focusing on and tackle the rest of the article or book at a later date. You might use only part of a book to provide you with insight into one aspect of your project or you might use one article you have obtained to direct you quickly to other papers on a subject.

Having completed one cycle of the literature survey process you will find that you are really just beginning. You may have uncovered more questions and misunderstandings than you started off with. You may feel that other issues, which you had not considered, appear to be influencing your project and justify further investigation. You may feel that you have been too broad with your initial aims and decide to focus on one particular aspect that interests you. Alternatively, you may feel that you were too focused on a particular issue and need to broaden your search. Whatever the case you will find that you are moving back into the cycle once again by refining and redefining your search for material. Once again, you may define your search explicitly or maintain a subjective understanding of material in which you are interested. The cycle thus proceeds as you continue to search and evaluate the literature, focusing ever more closely on information relevant to your project.

The 'spiralling in' effect apparent in Figure 4.5 represents your increased focus on the particular *topic* of interest. This is not to say that your search focuses in consistently over time as indicated in Figure 4.5. There are times when your search may broaden, but the focus on material relevant to your project will always improve. Thus, from a broad starting point, which might include books, journals, documentation, news reports and so on, you will find yourself drawn more and more towards specific articles relating directly to your project. Your literature review is therefore seen to 'evolve' over a period of time as you become more confident with the subject material and your conceptual understanding of the topic area increases.

This iterative process highlights the fact that the literature review is not something that you can write as a one-off having read everything you can get your hands on. It must develop over time. Although you will have to stop work on your literature survey at some point and move onto the main content of your project, you may well find that you are making changes to your literature review right up until the end. This will be inevitable as you should continue to gather and evaluate material throughout the lifetime of your project to keep your understanding of the field fresh and up-to-date.

4.3 Literature searching

A literature search is a '*systematic* gathering of *published* information relating to a subject' (University of Derby 1995). There are two important terms italicised within this statement that require further explanation. The first is *systematic*. A literature search should not be performed in an *ad hoc* manner, but should be approached in a structured and professional way. Reading anything and everything you come across will eventually be boring and will certainly be a waste of time. It is important to focus your literature search on those articles, books and so on that are relevant. Of course, when you first begin your literature search you won't know which material is relevant and which is extraneous. However, as you continue to cycle through the literature survey process, your focus will improve as your boundaries draw in towards your specific topic of interest. You should, therefore, identify your boundaries and know when to stop. Although this can be difficult at the start of your project, you should try to limit your search as much as possible. Knowing when to stop can also be hard as you will still have a lot of unanswered questions you may wish to solve before moving on to the main part of your project. However, remember that you will never actually stop literature searching as you might still be gathering/understanding material in parallel with the rest of your work to the conclusion of your project.

The second significant term within the definition is *published*. This implies that the material which you trace should be *recognised*. In other words, the material is not merely somebody's opinions you happened across through a conversation in a corridor, or a block of unrefereed text downloaded from the Internet. Recognised works are those that have been suitably *refereed* before publication. In other words, they have been assessed for their academic worth by other 'experts' in the field and accepted as significant artefacts that contribute to that field.

Bearing these two points in mind, there are also two golden rules you should remember when performing a literature search:

- Allow plenty of time – it can, and probably will, take a long time. Therefore, you should start as soon as possible, avoid procrastinating (see Chapter 5) and avoid gathering material unrelated to your chosen topic.
- Ensure that you make note of the full reference of any material you obtain. This will save a significant amount of time at the end of your project as you won't waste time trying to pin down precise details of articles you have read but have since lost or returned to your local library. The full reference will also be needed if you wish to apply for inter-library loans.

It is also worth noting that you should not be overwhelmed by the enormity of literature you might find on your topic. You need to be selective and focus in on precisely those articles and books that are specifically relevant to your work. If, however, you find several books and numerous articles that cover your specific subject area in detail, then it might mean that your subject aim is still too broad and you should focus even more.

When you are assessing whether a book is worth reading you should begin (obviously) with the title, move on to the contents listing and scan the index for keywords that are important to you. Is the author well recognised in his or her field? Is the book up-to-date? Is it the latest edition? When you are thinking of reading or obtaining an article, again, begin with the title and ask yourself if it is up-to-date or might it have been overtaken by now? Read the abstract and keywords, look at the list of references at the back (Are the key works cited? Are there useful references you can use?). Move on to reading the introduction and the summary/conclusions. Assess its level: is it highly technical, readable, is it a review paper, an introductory paper, a discussion paper? Only if you are satisfied that books and articles address all your needs should you read them from cover to cover. In many cases a select number of chapters in a book may be of use to you and only some sections of an article may be relevant.

Not only will your search require you to obtain literature on your chosen subject but it might also involve you searching for, identifying and obtaining suitable software for your project. For example, if your project is aiming to evaluate different software tools in different organisational environments you will need to ensure you have traced suitable, up-to-date tools for this evaluation. While software you obtain will not be used to justify and contextualise your project in a literature review, it may well be crucial for you to complete your project successfully. It is important, therefore, that you begin to search for and obtain this software as soon as possible and you may well find yourself pursuing this at the same time as your literature survey.

The points made above and the rules which you should follow provide you with a broad, subjective understanding of the nature of a literature search. In addition to these points you will need to understand the mechanics of the search. There are two aspects to this – understanding the format in which the information can be found and tracing this information. These two aspects are now discussed in turn.

4.3.1 *Format of information*

Literature is presented in a number of different formats. Some forms are more accessible than others and some are recognised as being more 'academically' valuable and worthy (see the points made on *recognised* works earlier). The following subsections give a summary of the forms of material you might come across during your literature search. The list is by no means exhaustive and for more details on these and other sources you should refer to texts such as Blaxter *et al.* (1996: 96–101), Saunders *et al.* (1997: 43–47) and Gash (1989).

Books

Books will probably prove to be the starting point for your literature survey. They will provide you with a good grounding and a good overview of your chosen topic area. However, remember that they may be outdated and out of line with current thinking in your field. Books are also written for different audiences, some being more technical than others. You should ensure that any books you acquire provide sufficient detail for your needs. Generally speaking, books *are* refereed and do provide a suitable basis for a literature survey.

Journals
Journals contain (normally refereed) articles discussing up-to-date issues in their field. You may find it daunting at first to read journal articles as they (should) represent the current limits and developments in your subject area. You may, therefore, find it easier to build a solid understanding in your chosen subject using books before attempting to investigate the latest developments and theories from journal articles.

Journal articles will also tend to be quite specific, focusing on developments in detailed aspects of a particular topic. You may find, then, as mentioned earlier, that only part of an article is suited to your needs.

As you continue your literature survey you should find yourself using journal articles more and more as your understanding of your subject becomes deeper. Indeed, when you complete your literature review you should find that the majority of references you make are to journal articles which represent the latest thinking in your field.

Conference proceedings
Conference proceedings contain articles and papers that have been presented at national and international conferences. The quality of articles in conference proceedings varies widely – some conferences are not refereed at all while others bring together the latest findings from internationally renowned experts in particular fields. Sometimes conference proceedings may contain more up-to-date ideas than you can find in journal articles and sometimes they present preliminary results from research that has yet to mature.

CD-ROM
Increasingly these days material is being presented on CD-ROMs. CD-ROMs really only present information from other sources in a more easily accessible format. For example, CD-ROMs contain varying types of information, from book-type material and conference proceedings to journal articles.

Company reports
Company reports and documentation can provide valuable information for case studies. However, care must be taken with these kinds of material as they might be subjectively biased in favour of the company and may contain information that you cannot use as the company does not wish it to be made public.

Theses
Theses are the published reports/dissertations of PhDs and MPhils. They will

represent the work of a postgraduate's project and provide a contribution in their particular field. Not only will they supply you with ideas on current thinking in a particular area but they will also provide a useful source of relevant references and, if you are a postgraduate student, an idea of the scope and requirements of a postgraduate degree. Having said that, theses are sometimes difficult to obtain – probably being lodged only at the awarding institution – although they can be obtained through inter-library loan.

Manuals

Particularly within technical computing projects, manuals may prove to be a valuable source of information. It might, for example, be impossible for you to perform your project without having access to the relevant technical manual. However, remember that they are just manuals, they are not refereed academic articles providing insight into current thinking in your field. You should treat manuals just as they are and not use them as foundations for academic discussion within your report.

Software

Any software that you require for your project, such as software tools, libraries and reusable components, should be obtained as soon as possible. You would not want to be halfway through your project and find that the software you needed was no longer available or too expensive. You may have identified some relevant software when you completed your project proposal (see the discussion of resource requirements in Section 2.3.3) but it is important that you obtain this as soon as you can. Sources you can use to trace relevant software include the Internet (using keyword searches and company web sites), local companies (who may well be using suitable software tools) and professional organisations. Professional organisations (such as the British Computer Society, the Project Management Institute and so on) often have *special interest groups* in particular areas, which can be contacted for help and information. This might include software reviews on tools used in their particular field of study and databases of companies supplying relevant software.

In addition to the above media you may also find material in forms such as video and microfiche. Treat these sources with the respect they deserve. For example, a refereed journal presented on microfiche is as valuable as a refereed journal on paper. An introductory video on your subject area may provide you with as good a grounding in your topic as an introductory text book.

Other sources of information that should be treated with more caution include letters and memos, newspapers, computing magazines, the Internet, company sales literature and television programmes. Newspapers, television programmes and computing magazines may provide popular material but their depth may be somewhat limited. However, computing magazines often discuss up-to-date technical issues and provide topical quotations from key orators for use in your report. Letters, memos and company sales literature will provide limited material and are likely to be quite biased.

The Internet may seem a valuable source of information but it must be treated with extreme caution. You can spend hours 'surfing' the Internet wasting time, without finding anything of value. In addition, material that you do trace might well be unqualified, unrefereed opinion that has no recognised grounding within your particular field of study. Data are also 'unstable', being updated and modified regularly. While this can be a good thing in that material is always up-to-date, it can mean that the information disappears quickly as well. Having said that, the Internet can prove to be a useful search tool for academically sound material, company information and software, and you can often find works published elsewhere (journal articles, for example) that are difficult to obtain through normal sources – for example, through digital library resources. Make sure if you do use any material from the Internet that you note the full web address of the material for referencing purposes. For more detail on how to use the Internet wisely for research purposes you can read Campbell and Campbell (1995), which is an entire book devoted to this topic.

4.3.2 *Tracing the information*

You now know the format that literature is presented in, but how do you actually trace these sources of information? The best place to start any literature search is in your own institution's library. You should also make good use of the librarians, who know the most efficient ways to trace particular sources of information within your institution. Detailed below are some examples of material you can use to trace literature on your subject. The list is by no means exhaustive and you should consult your own library and library staff for other search material they might have.

Internet

Although, as discussed earlier, you should be careful when using the Internet to access literature for your project, the Internet *is* a valuable tool for tracing articles and information. The Internet in this context refers to the use of web browsers (such as Netscape Navigator or Microsoft Internet Explorer) to access web *sites*. It is useful to employ some form of *search engine* when looking for particular items on the Internet. Two such engines can be accessed at:

> http://www.yahoo.co.uk/
> http://www.infoseek.com/

Web sites that prove useful for tracing information include those produced by publishers such as Elsevier Science, which publishes numerous journals. Elsevier provides a service whereby you are emailed with the contents listings of recent journals in which you are interested. Their Internet site can be accessed at:

http://www.elsevier.nl:80/

Through your connection to the Internet you will also be able to access *mailing lists* and *newsgroups*. Mailing lists are provided by *list servers* and are established to deal with particular subjects or special interest groups. By submitting your email address and subject interest(s) to a list server you will be added to the mailing list. You will then receive mailings from people on your particular subject of interest. This works by people submitting comments, questions, discussion points and so on to the list server, which are then forwarded to everyone on the mailing list. The messages that are forwarded are either moderated (checked by a human beforehand) or unmoderated (all messages are forwarded).

One such list server is Mailbase provided by the University of Newcastle upon Tyne. To find out more about this service, and the subject areas that are available, you can access the Mailbase web site at:

http://www.mailbase.ac.uk/

Newsgroups are similar to bulletin boards or notice boards. They cover an enormous range of topics from specific academic subject areas to general-interest 'chat' groups. The most common way to access newsgroups is through your own web browser. Your Internet Service Provider or university computer services department will be able to advise you on what groups are available locally and how this facility is supported.

OPAC

Most institutions these days have an OPAC (Online Public Access Catalogue) which you can use to perform searches for material held in your library. OPAC provides a far more efficient way of performing searches (be it on author's name, title, keywords and so on) than older, manual paper-based or microfiche-based systems. If your library has one of these systems you should learn how to use it.

You can also access OPACs at other institutions via the Internet. For example, the British Library OPAC can be accessed at:

http://opac97.bl.uk/

Most university OPACs can also be accessed via:

http://copac.ac.uk/copac/

or

http://www.niss.ac.uk/

BIDS

BIDS (Bath Information Data Services) is a database that contains up-to-date abstracts and article details from a number of scientific journals and conferences. The service is available by subscription and is usually provided on an institutional basis. It can be accessed via the Internet at:

> http://www.bids.ac.uk/

The BIDS service also provides an index to scientific and technical conference proceedings.

The following sources are also useful for tracing information:

- British National Bibliography: this provides a list of all British books published and deposited at the British Library each year. It is available in printed format and as a CD-ROM.
- British Books in Print: a microfiche listing all British books *currently* in print.
- American Books in Print: a microfiche listing all American books *currently* in print.
- Global Books in Print: a CD-ROM containing information on all books recently published in the USA, the UK, continental Europe, Africa, Asia etc.
- ASLIB: an index of PhD theses completed in the UK each year. It provides abstracts and is arranged in subject order.
- Current Research in Britain: a catalogue that presents, in institution order, research activity that is ongoing within UK universities. Computing research is covered within the physical sciences volumes. It is published annually.
- Index to Conference Proceedings: provides an index of conference proceedings received by the British Library. It is available in printed form or via the British Library web page.
- Computer Abstracts: a printed catalogue that provides abstracts and details of articles published from a number of computer journals, published every six months. It is also available via the Internet at:

    > http://www.anbar.co.uk:compabs/

- Computer Select: a CD-ROM that contains complete articles published monthly in a number of computer journals.
- ULRICHS: an international periodicals directory in printed format which provides details of journals published throughout the world.

Inter-library loans

Although your search can provide you with a comprehensive list of material that will support your project, there is no guarantee that your local library will stock the items you require. This is when you need to make use of the inter-library loans system. Your institution will be able to obtain material for you from other institutions using this system. However, the system has three potential drawbacks:

- It is expensive and often undergraduates will have to pay for this service.
- It can take some time before you receive an article you have ordered – possibly too long in some cases.
- You can be severely limited on how long you may keep the material (for example, one or two weeks when you may want a book for two or three months).

Having said this, the system is well worth using if you require pertinent articles and books for your project that are not available locally.

Some tips for performing a literature search
- Note interesting quotations and their reference as you go along.
- Use review articles and books to help your search.
- Reference correctly from the start (covered in Chapter 6).
- Know when to stop – or at least when to move on to the next stage of your project. You will know this from your project plan and the research boundaries which you have set yourself.
- Have a system to organise and catalogue the material you read – see below for a discussion on how to manage your information.
- Read recognised leaders and original theorists in your field.
- Start with a broad search before you focus in – don't jump straight into the most complicated recent article on your subject: you may be put off by its apparent complexity.

4.4 Managing information

Collecting a large number of articles and books relating to your subject is all very well but, depending on the size of your project and the breadth and depth of your literature search, you may soon find yourself swamped under paperwork and books. Some people manage to work well under these conditions, able to put their hands on a particular piece of paper under a pile of 'debris' on their desk. For the rest of us it makes sense to have some means of managing and controlling the literature and information gathered to avoid losing sight of important articles or losing references that are later needed. This section briefly introduces some tips and ideas to help you manage the articles, books and references you obtain from your literature search. For a more detailed discussion on managing research material you can read Orna and Stevens (1995).

The best way to begin managing your research is by using the conceptual model you have created of your subject area (using your RTM, relevance tree or spider diagram). Use this model to identify the topics in which you are interested and how these topics link together. You can use this model to sort articles and books that you obtain into some sort of order. Some articles may cover broad issues while others may draw together two or three important topics. Arrange photocopied articles and your own notes into plastic wallets or folders suitably labelled. In this way you will quickly and easily be able to draw together relevant information as you tackle different parts of your project.

Another important strategy to follow is to set up an index system of some kind that includes information on every article and book that you read. Some books that discuss literature searching will recommend that you set up a manual index system on cards. These days, however (and especially for computing students), it is better to use a computer to do this. It is quicker, less bulky, the information is readily available in a format which you can use (paste) in your final report, and it can be updated easily. You can use a word processor to record details of your references – such as title, keywords (for quick searching for similar topics), brief overview etc. Alternatively, there are software packages available that manage references for you. Examples of shareware packages include *References Manager 1.5* for the Apple Macintosh, *Nineveh* for Windows, and *REFLIST 2.0* for DOS. These packages are available via Internet archive sites such as HENSA at *http://www.hensa.ac.uk*. In addition there are commercial packages available, such as Reference Manager for Windows 98 (refer to *http://www.risinc.com* for more details).

Also, try to record references in the correct format from the start – this will enable you to use them directly when you complete your project later on. It is also a good idea to note the primary reference of each article you obtain; i.e. how did you discover that article in the first place? Was it referred to by another article you read or did you just come across it by chance as you searched the library shelves?

When you are reading articles highlight key phrases, sentences and paragraphs by underlining or using a highlighter pen. You may set up a system whereby you use a green pen to highlight useful quotations, orange to highlight explanations to key topics, pink to highlight new ideas or contributions, and blue to highlight contradictions or arguments with your way of thinking. In books you can use Post-it notes to quickly identify important pages and also enable you to make brief notes on the book at key points.

Another useful idea is to make brief notes on the front page of articles and within the papers themselves. This might provide an explanation to yourself of what the author is trying to say or to note another reference you feel is related to this particular point (whether it supports or contradicts the argument). You might like to provide your own brief summary of the paper at the start as well. This will save you having to reread the entire paper six months later when you have forgotten what it was all about and you are trying to incorporate it into your report.

These ideas will not provide you with a comprehensive information management system. This is something only you can develop based on your own way of working and your own feelings and ideas. However, the approaches discussed above will provide you with a useful basis, having introduced you to the key skills used by researchers to manage information.

4.5 Critical evaluation

You have gathered some articles and books together, have read them to some extent and have an idea of what each one is about and what the author is trying to say. How do you critically evaluate them?

Normally when people hear or read the word 'criticise' they think of it in a negative sense, i.e. finding fault with the object in question. However, to critically evaluate an article means far more than looking for faults – this is certainly not the aim of critical evaluation.

When you read an article or a book you should consider the following points. This is not to say that you should apply these points as a 'tick list' but you should be thinking about these ideas implicitly as you read the article. You should also try to think how the article can contribute to your own work.

- What kind of article is it – a review paper, an evalulatory paper, a theory paper, a practical paper, a case study etc.?
- What can you gain from the article – ideas, techniques, useful quotations etc.?
- Is the author well recognised in his or her field? Is he or she an authority in this area?
- What contribution is being made by the article? What kind of contribution is it? Can it make a contribution to your own project? If so, how?
- How does the article fit within its context? How does the article fit into and support the context of your project? How important is the article in its field and your own? Does the paper classify and summarise its field in a clearer or more logical way than has been done before?
- Do conclusions follow logically from the work that has been presented? Are the arguments logical? Do they follow one another? Are they supported or contradicted by the work of others? Are alternative conclusions consistent with the discussion?
- Can you differentiate fact from unsubstantiated opinion? If there are opinions in the article do you agree with them? Are these opinions supported by logical arguments or other authors?
- What do you feel about what has been written? Do you agree with statements that are made? Are there any counter arguments?
- Does the article contradict other viewpoints or support the status quo? How does the article relate to other literature in the field?

- What references does it use? Are these appropriate, relevant, up-to-date? Which references can you use? Is the article referred to by other authors?
- Are there limits to what the author is suggesting? Is his or her argument only applicable in certain cases?
- Can you use the results from the article in your own work? How do these results contribute and fit into their field and your own?

Rudestam and Newton (1992: 50) suggest some additional points that should be considered when reading and critically evaluating articles. They break their points down into five key areas: *conceptualisation, theoretical framework and hypotheses, research design, results and discussion*, and *summary*. Those that supplement the points made above and are applicable for computing projects can be summarised as:

- What is the major problem or issue being investigated?
- How clearly are the major concepts defined/explained?
- Is there a clear research question/hypothesis that can be, and is, tested?
- What type of research design/methodology is employed? Is it suitable and reliable?
- Have algorithms and statistical techniques been used appropriately? Can you apply them in your own work? What are the limitations of these techniques?
- Is the choice of measures, sample sizes and data appropriate? Have extraneous factors/variables been considered?
- Can generalisations be made from these results? What are the limitations of these generalisations?
- Are the implications of the results discussed?
- What is your overall assessment of the study in terms of its adequacy for explaining the research problem and the contribution it is making?

Taking all of these points into consideration, you will see that critical awareness of your chosen subject means a lot more than just understanding it and being able to regurgitate parts of it. Reading and understanding what you have read is really only the first part of the process. You should be aware of its boundaries, its limitations, contradictions, developing areas and dead ends. The main point of critical evaluation is that you *think* about what you are reading. This *critical reading* is defined by Blaxter *et al.* (1996: 106) using a number of points, some of which are listed below.

A critical reading is:

- 'one that goes beyond mere description by offering opinions, and making a personal response, to what has been written';
- 'one that relates different writings to each other';
- 'one that does not take what is written at face value';

- 'one that views research writing as a contested terrain, within which alternative views and positions may be taken up'.

Using these pointers as you read and interpret the material you obtain will ensure that you develop a deeper (not superficial) understanding of your subject area. You will be developing the depth of knowledge that will be expected on your degree course.

4.6 Writing literature reviews

You are now critically aware of your subject area and the literature in your chosen field. How do you present your understanding of your field and set the foundation for your project using the literature you have obtained as a literature review?

As a starting point for discussion, Borg and Gall (1989, cited by Saunders *et al.* 1997: 39) identify the purpose of a literature review as, among other things:

- to refine your research question and objectives;
- to highlight research possibilities that have either been explicitly identified by other authors or have possibly been overlooked in the past;
- to avoid repeating the work of others;
- to identify research methods and strategies that may be usefully applied in your own research.

Building on these points, a literature review should provide 'a coherent argument that leads to the description of a proposed study' (Rudestam and Newton 1992: 47). This is achieved with reference to past and current literature in your field(s) and will involve a discussion of current omissions and any biases you may have identified (Saunders *et al.* 1997). You will have great difficulty achieving these aims if you merely read and digest a number of articles and books related to your project. It is through your critical evaluation (discussed in the previous section) and critical understanding of the relevant literature that your literature review will develop.

You will not be able to write a literature review without reference to other material in the field. References should, therefore, be used to support your arguments *where appropriate*. They should not be used to pad out your report and 'prove' that you have read (or, at least, have obtained) a number of key texts.

There are no specific, infallible rules you can apply to write the perfect literature review. It is something that improves with practice and something that you can get a feel for by reading examples within the varied literature you will come across. However, at a 'mechanistic' level within project reports, Saunders *et al.* (1997: 40) identify three common ways for presenting literature reviews:

- as a single chapter;
- as a series of chapters;
- subsumed within the report as various issues are tackled.

For an undergraduate project it is unlikely (unless your entire project is a literature review) that you will dedicate a series of chapters to your literature review. Not only will you not have enough time to do this, but you will also not be expected to gather sufficient material to fill several chapters. It is more common for your report to contain an introductory chapter dedicated to a literature review or for you to subsume your review within each chapter of your report where you discuss different elements of your project. Quite clearly the approach you adopt is up to you and is something about which your supervisor should advise you.

When writing your literature review remember what it is not:

- It is not a report that lists all the papers and books you have read whether they are relevant or not. You must be selective about that to which you refer.
- It must not dedicate a page or paragraph to each article in turn, merely reporting on their content. Haywood and Wragg (1982: 2) refer to this as 'the furniture sales catalogue, in which everything merits a one-paragraph entry no matter how skilfully it has been conducted'.

Perhaps the best way to explain the presentation of a literature review is through a small example. The box represents a short introduction to an academic paper. Quite clearly, academic papers of only two or three thousand words are much shorter than an entire project report. However, the example shows how the scene is set for the rest of the paper and its context is justified with respect to other literature in the field.

An artificial neural network approach to rainfall-runoff modelling

The United Nations General Assembly declared the 1990s the International Decade for Natural Disaster Reduction with the specific intent to disseminate existing and new information related to measures for the assessment, prediction, prevention and mitigation of natural disasters (WMO 1992). A prominent element within this programme has been the development of operational flood forecasting systems. These systems have evolved through advances in mathematical modelling (Wood and O'Connell 1985; O'Connell 1991; Lamberti and Pilati 1996), the installation of telemetry and field monitoring equipment at critical sites in drainage networks (Alexander 1991), through satellite and radar sensing of extreme rainfalls (Collier 1991), and through the coupling of precipitation and runoff models (Georgakakos and Foufoula-Georgiou 1991; Franchini *et al.* 1996). However, in practice, successful real-time flood forecasting often depends on the efficient integration of all these separate activities (Douglas and Dobson 1987). Under the auspices of the World Meteorological Organisation (1992) a series of projects were implemented to compare the characteristics and performance of various operational models and their updating procedures. A major conclusion of the most recent intercomparison exercise was the need for robust simulation models in order to achieve consistently better results for longer lead times even when accompanied by an efficient updating procedure.

The attractiveness of Artificial Neural Networks (ANNs) to flood forecasting is threefold. First, ANNs can represent any arbitrary non-linear function given sufficient complexity of the trained network. Second, ANNs can find relationships between different input samples and, if necessary, can group samples in analogous fashion to cluster analysis. Finally, and perhaps most importantly, ANNs are able to generalise a relationship from small subsets of data while remaining relatively robust in the presence of noisy or missing inputs, and can adapt or learn in response to changing environments. However, despite these potential advantages, ANNs have found rather limited application in hydrology and related disciplines. For example, French *et al.* (1992) used a neural network to forecast rainfall intensity fields in space and time, while Raman and Sunilkumar (1995) used an ANN to synthesise reservoir inflow series for two sites in the Bharathapuzha basin, S. India.

The use of artificial neural networks for flood forecasting is an area which has yet to be fully explored. Up until now the majority of work in this area has been mainly theoretical; concentrating on neural network performance with artificially generated rainfall-runoff data; for example Minns and Hall (1996). However, these theoretical approaches tend to overlook the difficulty in converting and applying actual data to artificial neural network topologies. Hall and Minns (1993) go some way to address this criticism by applying neural networks to a small urban catchment area. However, their discussion is limited to the performance of a neural network on a small number of events.

This paper goes one stage further by discussing how artificial neural networks may be developed and used on 'real' hydrological data. It discusses the problems that need to be addressed when applying neural networks to rainfall-runoff modelling and demonstrates the effectiveness of artificial neural networks in this particular domain. By applying a neural network to flood simulation in two UK catchments, the prospects for the

> use of ANNs in real-time flood forecasting are evaluated. Finally, suggestions are made concerning necessary refinements to the existing ANN prior to transfer to operational use.

Source: reproduced in part from Dawson and Wilby (1998)

Notice how this introduction/literature review begins by justifying the content of the paper with reference to a WMO report. It continues by showing how the subject area has evolved over the years. Literature reviews often employ this kind of approach – focusing on the topic of interest through a chronological discussion of literature in the field. This approach generally leads to a natural focus on the topic of concern. The review then moves on to explain a little bit more about the area of study, setting the scene for the reader, before focusing more precisely and discussing some recent developments in research within the field. The literature review concludes by highlighting current limitations in the field, once again justifying the relevance and importance of the paper by showing how it aims to fill these gaps.

In summary, literature reviews evolve over a period of time. They cannot be written as one-offs, after you have read a few articles on your chosen subject. Although you will not split your literature review into specific sections your review should, implicitly, justify the existence of your project (by critically evaluating past and current research in the field), identify your project within a wider context, and discuss and arrange relevant literature in the field. In other words, your literature review forms the *foundation* of your project.

4.7 Summary

- Your literature survey will help to place your project within a wider context and justify its presence within a particular field (or fields) of study.
- Your literature survey consists of two main components: the literature search (supported by an ability to manage the information you gather) and the literature review (which requires a critical understanding of material which you obtain). These components are performed repetitively over a period of time and (probably) in parallel with one another.
- Although you will eventually need to move on to the main investigation/development work of your project, your literature survey will continue to be performed throughout the lifetime of your project to some extent, as you refine and consolidate the information you gather, ensuring that your project remains up-to-date.

4.8 Further reading

Blaxter, L., Hughes, C. and Tight, M. (1996) *How to Research*, Open University Press, Buckingham.
Campbell, D. and Campbell, M. (1995) *The Student's Guide to Doing Research on the Internet*, Addison-Wesley, Wokingham.
Gash, S. (1989) *Effective Literature Searching for Students*, Gower, Aldershot.
Rudestam, K.E. and Newton, R.R. (1992) *Surviving Your Dissertation*, Sage, London.
Saunders, M., Lewis, P. and Thornhill, A. (1997) *Research Methods for Business Students*, Pitman, London.

CHAPTER 5
Doing your project

Aims
To introduce the skills needed to manage yourself and your project effectively as it is progressing.

Learning objectives
When you have completed this chapter, you should be able to:

- understand the main elements of projects that require managing and controlling;
- control your project as it progresses;
- understand problems that can occur and be aware of ways of dealing with them;
- manage your time more effectively;
- know how to make effective use of your supervisor;
- work efficiently in a project team.

5.1 Introduction

Although you may have proposed an interesting and worth while project and planned it well, once your project is under way it needs to be carefully managed and controlled or it *will* fall apart. You cannot assume that, having completed a detailed project plan and a solid literature survey, the project itself will be plain sailing and you can relax. You need to be aware of problems that might arise, you need to remain motivated, you need to manage your time effectively, and you need to make effective use of your supervisor. This chapter deals with these issues.

5.1.1 *Managing five project elements*

In any project, be it a large industrial development or your own academic computing project, there are a maximum of five elements that need to be managed and controlled as the project is progressing;

- Time
- Cost
- Quality
- Scope
- Resources

Within academic projects students will often argue that *time* is the most important of these elements. It is an element which you will always seem to be in need of. In virtually all academic projects you are limited in the amount of time you are allocated and, consequently, it has limited flexibility that you can control. All you can really do with respect to this element is to manage the time you have more efficiently – generally speaking, you cannot increase the amount of time you have available.

Cost is another factor over which you have little control. However, in most academic computing projects cost is not usually a concern. All the facilities you require are generally available; if they aren't, then your project would probably not have been accepted in the first place. If you require additional hardware, software or literature material you will either be provided with these or not – it is probably beyond your control.

The next two project elements – *quality* and *scope* – are those over which you have most control and, appropriately, have the greatest responsibility for. Quality refers to the quality of your project itself. How good is it? Is it at the right level (postgraduate or undergraduate level)? Is it of an acceptable standard for your course? Is it worth an Honours degree or just a Pass degree?

Whereas quality can be measured by the depth of your project (for example, how well you develop or investigate a particular aspect of study), *scope* is an indication of its breadth. In some ways scope is often viewed as an attribute of quality. It represents the final outcome of your project, what it actually achieves, its contribution, limits and magnitude.

The last element in the list, *resources*, is probably the most important one of all. Without resources there will be no project. In this case interest falls on the human resources that are available – that is you, your supervisor and possibly a project team. Making effective use of your supervisor is discussed in Section 5.4. In some cases you might be working in teams where colleagues need organising, tasks need to be assigned, and people's contributions drawn together. Working in teams is the subject of Section 5.5. For individual projects, organising yourself boils down to your ability to manage your own time. Managing time is discussed in Section 5.3.

Figure 5.1 emphasises the leading role resources play with all these five elements – shown at the crown of the diagram. It is through your own organisation that the elements within your project are balanced with respect to each other and with respect to your project's aims and objectives. The figure emphasises the fact that each of these elements is related to all the others in some way and

84 DOING YOUR PROJECT

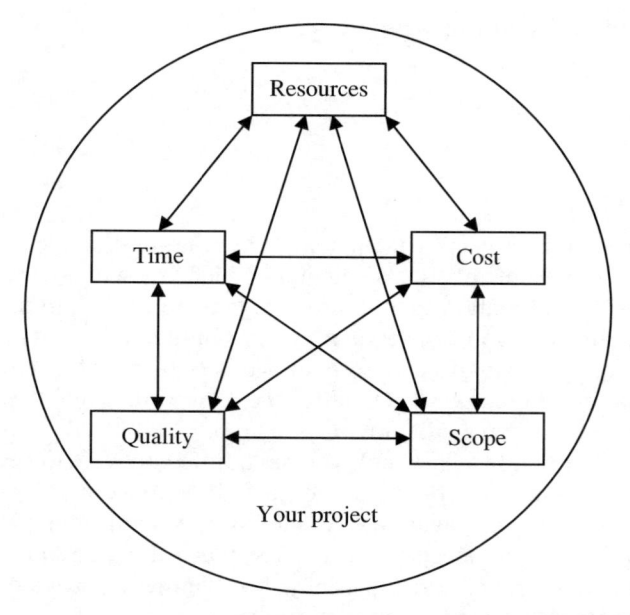

Figure 5.1 *Balancing the five project elements against one another*

tradeoffs can be made between them. How these tradeoffs are made as you monitor and control your project is discussed in the following section.

5.1.2 **Project control**

The five project elements require managing and controlling through the five main project stages identified in Chapter 3: definition, planning, initiation, control and closure. Focus on these five elements will change as your project progresses through these stages. For example, at your project's inauguration you won't be too concerned about time and will probably concentrate on your project's scope. During this stage you will feel that there is an eternity before the final report is due to be handed in. You may have many ideas you want to pursue and you might wish to investigate and develop various aspects within the field of computing. However, two weeks before you are due to submit your dissertation, time will suddenly become a very rare commodity and a real concern to you.

As your project progresses into the initiation and control stages emphasis moves from project management activities to product oriented activities. In other words you will begin to focus on the actual work of your project itself and direct your efforts towards investigating, developing and producing your project's deliverable, whatever you have identified this to be.

As your project progresses through these working stages you will still need to perform certain project management activities. You should, for example, monitor and control all your project's elements with respect to your project plan. You will control time by checking to see if you are completing tasks in line with the times planned on your Gantt chart. If you are, you are on schedule and should have no worries. If not, you might be falling behind schedule and you will need to do something about it. Not only should you monitor time as your project is progressing, but you should also keep an eye on your project's scope and quality. Are you, for example, meeting the objectives of your project satisfactorily or have you had to make some compromises along the way?

Project management will often involve deciding how to trade each of the five project elements off against one another as your project progresses. For example, you could reduce the scope of your project in order to improve its quality. Conversely, you may decide to expand the scope of your project (for example, by increasing the functionality of a program you are writing) at the expense of some quality (by introducing more bugs). Time is always limited so you will often find yourself trying to trade it with other elements – for instance, saving time by reducing quality and/or scope, particularly towards the end of your project. However, you must always ensure that you do not compromise your project and submit, on time, what you feel has been your best effort.

5.2 Dealing with problems

If your project progresses to completion smoothly, without any problems, you are probably very lucky indeed. Virtually all projects encounter problems at one stage or another, whether they are performed by leading academics at the cutting edge of science, first-year undergraduate students pursuing a small assignment, or large industrial project teams whose work can last for several years. It is not really the nature of the problem that you encounter that can lead to project failure, *but how you deal with the problem that counts.*

The key to successfully overcoming any problems is not to panic, tackle them objectively and professionally and make the best of the situation. Problems don't necessarily solve themselves and will often require some action from you in order to be resolved. The following five points encapsulate perhaps the most likely problems you will encounter when performing your academic project, with suggestions on how they might be overcome.

5.2.1 *Weakening*

Weakening is something that can happen at any stage of your project. It can stem from a lack of motivation, losing your direction, or the feeling that you have attempted to do far too much in the time available. Weakening is something that can usually be traced right back to the first stage of your project – its *definition*. Did you decide to pursue a project you weren't really interested in? When you planned your project did you plan to do too much? Were the aims and objectives of your project a little vague, leading you to lose faith in what you are doing because you don't appear to be heading anywhere?

The first solution to dealing with this problem is clearly to address its root cause, i.e. tackle it at your project's outset. Make sure that you select a topic which you are really interested in, define and plan it thoroughly and ensure that you have planned some flexibility into your project so that you can expand or contract its scope depending on the time that is available. This last point can also help to address weakening that is caused because you feel you are trying to do too much. Think about ways to reduce the scope of your project without compromising its quality. Alternatively, deal with large chunks of work by breaking them down into smaller more manageable pieces.

Another way to overcome a lack of motivation towards your work is to move on to something different. It may be that you are getting bogged down with a particular part of your project and working at too fine a level of detail. Try to identify from your project plan other areas of work you can do. You may then return to the area you are struggling with later when you are refreshed from your break. Other ways to deal with weakening are addressed in Section 5.3, on time management, where *procrastination* is discussed.

5.2.2 **Personal problems**

Over the period of your project, be it six months, a year or whatever, the chances are that you will experience a personal incident of one kind or another. This can range from happy occasions such as getting married, having a baby and so on, to sadder, more difficult events to cope with such as illness, family bereavement, splitting up with your partner etc. Other personal 'problems' you might encounter include moving house or changing jobs. These kinds of changes might be good or bad but one thing is certain, they will be a drain on your time and your emotional energies. Although it is beyond the scope of this book to discuss how you deal with these problems from an emotional level, their impact on your project and what you can do to deal with this impact is of concern.

The most important thing to do in any of these situations is to tell somebody what has happened – your supervisor, personal tutor, course leader etc. Your own institution should have guidelines on who to approach first with problems of different natures and you should try to follow these suggestions. You may then be guided towards other departments within the university which can deal more effectively with your difficulties: the students' union, counselling services, local doctors, hospital, chaplaincy and so on.

The chances are that your institution will also operate some form of 'extenuating circumstances' procedures. These procedures enable you to inform your institution officially of what has happened, enabling them to consider how to deal with you and possibly how to help you with your project. This will probably involve completing a form and providing evidence of some kind, such as a doctor's note. Note, however, that your institution will have guidelines on what is an acceptable reason for claiming extenuating circumstances – such as illness – and what is not – for example, going on a holiday with your friends for two months.

By following your institution's procedures you are at least going some way to dealing with your problem. Not only will they be able to help you on an emotional level (for example, with counselling services) but you may well be awarded extensions to complete your work. Above all, remember that if you do not let anyone know what has happened then nothing can be done to help.

5.2.3 *Computer failure*

In almost all projects these days, computers are used to a greater or lesser extent. They might be used simply to word process your final report or they might be used throughout the entirety of your project as you develop a program or use them to analyse data. Whatever the case you may well find that the computer you use fails and that data and files you are using are lost or erased forever.

The only answer to these kinds of problems is to make numerous and frequent backups. These can be made onto floppy disks, so you can take them away with you, or onto your institution's own file server. These days, other media, such as CD-ROMs and Zip drives, can also be used. It is up to you how often and how many backup copies you make – you know how reliable the system you are using is. However, to make no backups at all is ill advised. Certainly, towards the end of your project, daily backups will be essential. Losing an entire week's work at the start of your project is not too serious, but at the end it would be disastrous. Take the example in the box as a cautionary tale.

> John was a final year undergraduate student on a computer studies course at the time when network accounts were rare and everyone kept their work on floppy disks which they carried around with them. He was reasonably well organised and as such made three backup copies of his work every day. One day when he was working on his dissertation he found that he couldn't read any data on one of his disks. Fortunately, he had his backup disks with him and loaded one of these into the machine he was using. Once again the computer claimed the disk was unreadable.
>
> What had happened was the disk drive itself was broken and was erasing any disks that were inserted into it. Had John made only one backup of his work he would have lost everything. Fortunately, with three backups, all was not lost and he was able to complete his project on time.

5.2.4 Data availability

Data availability is often a problem with computing projects. Either a journal or a book you require is unavailable, you can't get hold of some data, you lose your contact in a local company where you hoped to perform a case study, or you receive a poor response from some questionnaires you issued. Whatever the problem, your project looks as though it will suffer from a lack of available data.

In a similar vein to *weakening*, discussed earlier, problems with data availability can often be traced back to your project's early stages. If you had thought about your project more thoroughly during its inauguration, you might have identified that a book or journal was difficult to obtain, questionnaires were likely to prove unreliable and so on. Bearing these things in mind you might well set up contingency plans at an early stage – for example, changing your project's direction so that it doesn't require data x, y or z.

If, however, data availability problems only become apparent well into your project they must be dealt with there and then. Simply put, either the data are available or they are not. In other words, can you obtain the information you require from any other source? If not, then move on without them. Is there another company you could use as a case study? Have you time to chase up the questionnaires or send out new ones? You should try to think of as many alternatives as you can and your supervisor should be able to help you. If not, you will have to proceed without these data and adjust your project accordingly. This is, perhaps, easier said than done. However, if at the end of the day the data are unavailable, you cannot conjure the data from nowhere and the sooner you accept this, adjust and proceed with your project the better.

5.2.5 Other things taking priority

Your computing project will never be (and shouldn't be) your only interest. You will have other subjects to deal with – coursework, your part-time or full-time job, a social life, a personal life and so on. All of these things take time and often you will find that your project takes second place to all of them at one stage or another. The only way to deal with this problem is through better time management. This is the subject of the following section.

5.3 Managing your time

Everybody is limited in the amount of time they have available – there are only 24 hours in a day and 7 days in a week, no matter who you are. Although everyone needs to use some of this time for essential activities such as sleeping, eating and dressing (referred to here as *essential* time), some people make more effective use of the remaining *serviceable* time than others. How you become more efficient in your use of serviceable time is the focus of *time management*.

Although there are some specific techniques you can employ to save time, the only way to make dramatic improvements in your use of time is to approach time management from a fundamental analysis. This fundamental analysis is a process that involves three stages and is summarised in Figure 5.2:

1. Decide what you want to do;
2. Analyse what you are currently doing;
3. Change what you are doing to achieve your aims.

Many people might try to improve their use of time by employing specific techniques that are identified in the third stage of this process. However, failure to comprehend your existing use of time, by omitting stages one and two of this process, will lead to only minor improvements in your time usage.

Each of these stages is now addressed in turn before presenting a summary of some specific ideas that can help you improve your use of time.

5.3.1 Deciding what you want to do

The first stage of successful time management is to decide exactly what you want to achieve in terms of goals and objectives. Most time management texts and courses will recommend that you identify both your short-term and long-term goals as part of this process. Short-term goals represent those things that you want to achieve during the following year. Long-term goals stretch much further into your future, such as five, ten or twenty years hence. For the purposes of this book the main focus is your short-term goals and it is assumed that completing your computing project is one of these goals.

It is far easier to categorise your goals according to their different types, rather than just attempting to identify broad objectives you are aiming for. Ferner (1980: 11) defines four categories you can use to identify your goals: *work goals, family goals, community goals* and *self goals*. Thus, if you were to

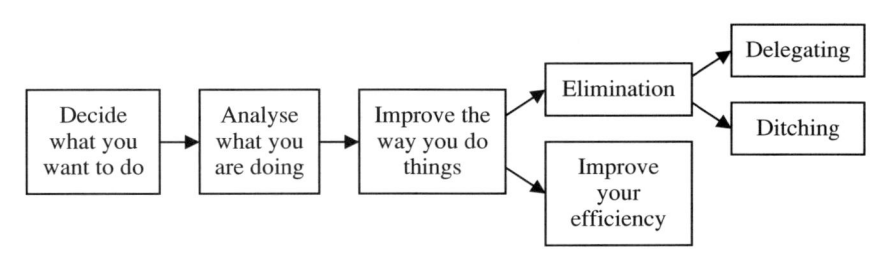

Figure 5.2 *The time management process*

categorise your goals for the year ahead, they might include targets such as:

- Work goals — Complete my degree with at least an upper second
- Family goals — Start a family
  Teach my children to swim
  Decorate the spare bedroom
- Community goals — Help out at the local youth club
  Train the local football team
  Do a sponsored walk for charity
- Self goals — Achieve grade 5 piano
  Get my golf handicap down to 10
  Learn to swim
  Join a local quiz team
  Complete a marathon
  Go on holiday to Hawaii

The goals you identify should be as specific as possible. For example, rather than just identifying a self goal as 'be happy', you should identify how you will achieve this, for example, 'go on holiday to Hawaii', 'get married' etc.

In Chapter 2, when project planning was introduced, how you should identify objectives that are steps towards your project's ultimate aim or goal was discussed. The same is true here. For example, one of your goals for the following year is to complete your degree course successfully (i.e. with at least an upper second). To achieve this goal you need to complete a number of objectives: complete your computing project successfully, pass your exams in subjects x, y and z, complete assignments a, b and c and so on. You are thus identifying that your computing project is something that is important to you. Just like all the other activities and events on your list of goals, it is identified as something to which you wish to commit yourself and something that you are willing to spend your time pursuing.

In this stage of the time management process you have identified the things that you hope to achieve. The next stage of the process involves checking to see what you are doing to see if you are really spending your time efficiently on the things you should be in order to achieve these goals.

5.3.2 Analyse what you are doing

Analysing how you are currently spending your time is achieved through two activities. First, you need to identify *how* you are spending your time and, second, you need to *categorise* the time you have identified. There are a number of techniques that you can use to identify your use of time, each technique doing much the same thing but in a slightly different way. *Time logs*, which are probably the most popular technique for recording time usage, are introduced here.

Time logs are simply lists that you make during the day of how you spend your time. They identify the activities you perform during the day, how long you spend on them, how efficient you were at performing them and, perhaps, ways in which you can improve your use of that time in future. You should continue making time logs for about a week to see if any patterns emerge. An example of a 'typical' day's time log is shown in Table 5.1.

This is perhaps an extreme example of a 'day in the life of'. You should also remember that this is just a snapshot of one day; this student may well be doing other things differently on other days of the week. This is why you should use time logs for a full week as individual days may provide spurious indicators of your time use.

Having a look through this time log can certainly help to identify some room for improvement (depending on the person's goals). If this student's main goal is to socialise then their use of time is probably quite effective. However, if they wish to do well in their exams and assignments, then some adjustments need to be made.

Table 5.1 A 'typical' daily time log

Time	Activity	Effectiveness	Comments/improvements
7.00–8.00	Get ready for university	50%	Could probably do this in 30 minutes but I'm always tired
8.00–8.30	Walk to campus	80%	Could get the bus but I need the exercise
8.30–9.00	Meet friends in canteen	10%	Need to socialise
9.00–10.00	Lecture	70%	Quite good today!
10.00–10.15	Coffee break	10%	I need a break
10.15–12.00	Tutorial/seminar	50%	Could have done this in half the time
12.00–1.30	Lunch – students' union	20%	Far too long but I need to eat
1.30–2.00	Library hunting for books	40%	Couldn't use the OPAC
2.00–2.30	Meeting with project supervisor	80%	Useful
2.30–3.00	Coffee with friends	20%	Need to socialise
3.00–4.00	Library hunting for books	20%	Not finding what I want
4.00–4.30	30 minutes on assignment	30%	Wasted time getting started – should spend longer on this
4.30–5.00	Walk home	80%	As before
5.00–5.30	Have a coffee	0%	No comment
5.30–6.00	Watch 'Neighbours'	0%	No comment
6.00–7.00	Get tea	50%	I need to eat
7.00–8.00	Work on assignment	90%	Get a lot done
8.00–11.00	Go to pub	40%	I need to socialise but should have done more work first
11.00–1.00	Work on project then go to bed	50%	Too tired to achieve much – must tackle this kind of thing earlier in the day

One important outcome from your daily time analysis is to identify your work performance. During the course of a day you will find that there are times when you work more effectively than others; for example, early in the morning, late at night and so on. You can plot these daily 'rhythms' on a work performance chart such as that shown Figure 5.3. Figure 5.3 shows that this person works more effectively during the morning and early in the evening than at any other time of day. Thus, it would be better for this person to schedule difficult tasks during these peak periods (for example, reading journal articles), and schedule easier tasks for other times. You can extend this concept to weekly work performance charts. For example, you may find that you work more effectively on Tuesdays and Wednesdays than Friday afternoons. Consequently, you will schedule your weekly work to coincide with this performance.

Having identified how you are spending your time, you should then categorise your use of serviceable time. Time is categorised, according to the goals you identified earlier, into the following two components: important/ unimportant and urgent/non-urgent. Table 5.2 summarises these categories.

Important activities are those activities that are important *to you* based on

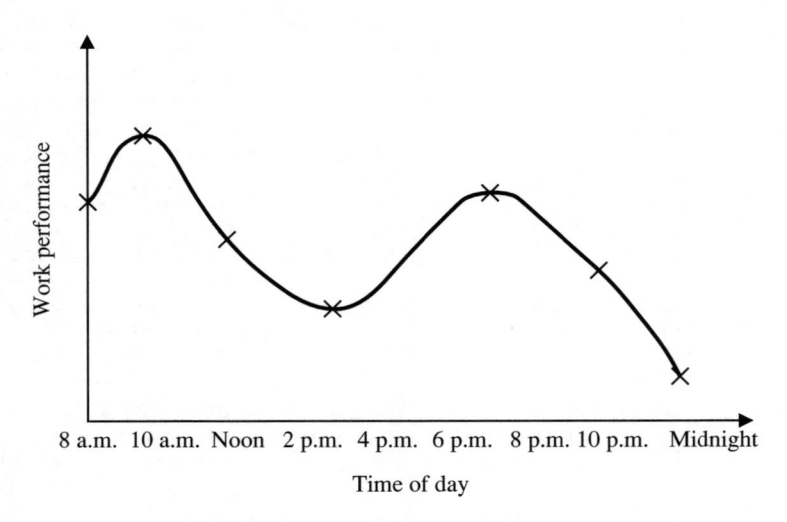

Figure 5.3 *A daily work performance chart*

Table 5.2 *Categories of time use (adapted from Jones, 1998: 62)*

	Important	Unimportant
Urgent	Do	Minimise/avoid
Non-urgent	Don't ignore	Abandon

your own goals and objectives, while unimportant activities are those that will not affect your goals and objectives if you don't do them. Urgent activities are those that must be done now and will not wait, while non-urgent activities are those that you could put off until tomorrow without causing any serious consequences.

Note that Table 5.2 only covers serviceable time. *Essential* time, which is time that you need to spend on essential day-to-day activities such as sleeping, eating, washing, dressing and food shopping, is not covered by these categories. Essential activities must be performed in order for you to function properly and to sustain you for everything else. However, although quite a number of activities you perform may appear essential, you might find that you could reduce the time you spend on them to some extent; for example, by taking shorter lunch breaks or getting someone else to do your shopping for you and so on.

All the activities you identify in your daily and weekly time log will fall into one of these categories. For example, completing an assignment that is due the following day would be important *and* urgent. At the start of the year your computing project would be important but at that stage it wouldn't be urgent. However, it would certainly become urgent towards the end of the year as its deadline approached.

An example of unimportant and non-urgent activities might be surfing the Internet or sorting your books into alphabetical order. Urgent and unimportant activities might include answering the phone, being interrupted by visitors, attending a meeting and so on.

Important and urgent activities are those which you must do and you must do now. If none of these activities is pending then you should focus on important and non-urgent ones. You should certainly avoid any activities that are unimportant and non-urgent and you should try to minimise, as much as possible, activities that are urgent but unimportant.

5.3.3 Change the way you do things

> What you can't dump, *delay*. What you can't delay, *delegate*. What you can't dump or delay or delegate, *do*.
>
> Turla and Hawkins (1985: 63)

There are only two ways to improve your use of time to achieve the goals you have set yourself:

1. eliminate activities you don't need to do;
2. be more efficient doing the things you have to do.

You can only eliminate activities in one of two ways. First, if they are unimportant, you can ditch them and should do so straight away. Second, if they are important, you might be able to delegate them to somebody else. For example, you may be able to persuade your partner or a friend to proofread your dissertation for you or help you trace some references in the library.

If you cannot eliminate tasks, you are left with only one option – become more efficient in doing the things you have to do. This is achieved by planning how best to use your time and dealing effectively with any problems that do arise. Planning how to use your time is usually done at two levels: weekly and daily. The first stage to time planning, however, is to set your priorities. The activities you need to perform on a daily and weekly basis are prioritised according to the categories introduced earlier (adapted from Ferner 1980: 118):

- High priority – must do – urgent and important;
- Medium priority – should do – important but not (yet) urgent;
- Low priority – nice to do – unimportant and non-urgent;
- Scheduled – low/medium/high priority scheduled activities – for example, meetings.

Weekly planning is best done either first thing on Monday morning or last thing on Friday. When planning what you want to achieve during the week ahead you will focus on high priority activities. You should schedule time during the week ahead to deal with high priority work and identify what you want to complete by the end of the week. Only when these activities are completed can you think about medium priority work. During the course of a week and during each day you will have scheduled events to deal with. Once again, only attend to these if they are medium or high priority. Try to avoid attending scheduled low priority events if you can.

Having decided what you want to achieve during the week you should plan what you want to achieve each day. Make a list of things you must do, scheduled activities for that day and things you can do if you find you have some free time available. Make sure that you allow plenty of time for high and medium priority tasks and schedule your day according to your daily work rhythms (see Figure 5.3). Try not to be too rigid with daily plans as unexpected events always arise and you should allow flexible time to deal with these things.

Although you may plan your weekly and daily time commitments thoroughly, there are always problems and unexpected events that occur. These are addressed in the following section.

5.3.4 *Dealing with problems*

Procrastination
Procrastination means that you put off until tomorrow what you can or should be doing today. The same might happen tomorrow and things that you ought to be doing never get done properly. There are various reasons why you might procrastinate – you have lost your motivation, the task appears too great, you

don't want to trouble somebody, you are nervous of the response you might get, and so on.

There are various ways you can deal with procrastination. The first thing to do is to decide that you really do want to deal with it. If this is difficult you can make a list on a piece of paper of the reasons for and against dealing with it. By breaking it down in this way you often convince yourself that the benefits of dealing with the task outweigh the negatives. If the task appears too great then the obvious answer is to break it down into manageable chunks and deal with each of these in turn.

Other ways you can deal with procrastination include the carrot and stick approach. Get somebody to monitor your progress – a colleague, your partner, a friend, your supervisor – and ask them to keep prompting you for progress reports on your work. Quite often, if you can't do work for yourself, knowing that someone else is interested in your progress does help. Another alternative is to reward yourself. Promise yourself some kind of treat if you complete the work – a trip to the cinema, a meal out or whatever.

Grains of time
Grains of time are those small periods of time you gain during the day that you don't use effectively – for example, waiting for someone to turn up to a meeting, finding your tutorial has been cancelled, sitting on the bus to college for half an hour, and so on.

Make sure that you don't waste these grains. Have something that you can pick up quickly and do to fill these periods – for example, some revision notes with you that you can read on the bus, a notebook so that you can jot down some ideas, the morning's post that you can sort through etc.

Unfinished business
It may appear obvious, but until a task is completed it is never actually finished. Don't start things that you will not finish. All the time you commit to half completing a task is wasted unless you finish that activity off.

Interruptions
Everyone is subject to interruptions to their work of one kind or another – people calling in to see you, the phone ringing, people asking you to do things, and so on. Some of these are unavoidable but it is how you deal with them that counts. One way to deal with interruptions is to avoid them by finding a 'hide away'. This might be a quiet place in your university's library where you know you won't get disturbed. You might want to put a notice on your door saying 'do not disturb' or go away for the weekend to get away from it all. If you do find that you are constantly being asked to do things you also need to learn to say 'no'. Don't deal with junk mail – just bin it. Remember your priorities, and if your computing project is due in, you must avoid doing other things and focus all your energies on it.

Perfectionism
Don't fall into the trap of trying to be perfect at everything you do. It can take a lot of time to improve something you do from 'good enough' to perfect. This time is wasted. For example, if you need to reply to a letter, don't waste two hours drafting out and redrafting a reply on a complex word processor with figures, clever fonts and letter heads. If you can, write a brief reply on the letter itself and post that back. If a brief reply is all that is required, do it.

Losing things
You can often waste a lot of time through your own inefficiency with data and files. Keep things in good order, references up-to-date, and have a means of managing all your paperwork. Gather together things you will need for a task before you start work. This will stop you interrupting your concentration and wasting time getting back 'up-to-speed' when you return. An additional tip here is to make a note of where you are up to and what you intend to do next when you have finished your work for the day. This will save time later when you try to remember what you were intending to do next.

5.4 Using your supervisor

5.4.1 *What is a supervisor?*

> A supervisor's principal professional responsibility is to help his or her research students to develop into individuals who think and behave as academic researchers in the field of study concerned.
>
> Cryer (1996: 59)

One of the main resources of your project is your supervisor and, as such, your relationship with him or her and your use of him or her needs managing effectively. Chapter 2 discussed some ideas on how you should choose your supervisor (if this is possible within your own institution) and what to look for in a supervisor. The purpose of this section is to discuss ways in which you can make effective use of your supervisor during the course of your project.

Although most institutions have similar guidelines for the supervisor/student relationship at postgraduate level, at undergraduate level institutions have quite different rules, expectations, roles and responsibilities for supervisors. Some institutions will expect you to work very closely with your supervisor, perhaps meeting with him or her regularly each week during the course of your project. Other institutions prefer to emphasise the independent nature of undergraduate project study and would only expect you to see a supervisor on rare occasions for advice and guidance. The role of your supervisor can also differ. Blaxter *et al.* (1996: 124) identify two roles that a supervisor can perform:

- A manager
- An academic advisor

As a *manager* your supervisor is responsible for managing your project in 'a more general sense'. He or she will be concerned with your overall progress. Are you meeting the milestones you have set for yourself? Are you coping with and balancing your project with other commitments? Your supervisor will also be concerned with ensuring you are following institutional guidelines as part of this role. For example, are you aware of all the guidelines and regulations relating to your project? Are you producing the right documentation at the right time? As a manager you may want your supervisor to encourage you when you are weakening, advise you on which procedures to follow to submit your dissertation, arrange access to particular hardware and software for you and so on.

As an *academic advisor* your supervisor is more concerned with the 'academic' content of your project. Are you reading the right journals and books? Are you following the correct research and data gathering methods? Are you performing the right analyses? Are you developing your software in the correct way? You may need your supervisor's academic expertise to advise you where to go next, what areas to develop further, to clarify particular topics and advise you which techniques and tools to use.

Blaxter *et al.* (1996: 126, citing University of Warwick 1994: 24) list the following areas which your supervisor should be able to advise you on when acting in an academic capacity:

- research design and scheduling;
- literature surveys;
- theoretical and conceptual development;
- methodological issues;
- development of appropriate research skills;
- data collection and analyses.

Sometimes you will also need your supervisor to act in a *pastoral role* for you. Under this role your supervisor will be more concerned with your emotional and general well being. Are you maintaining your motivation? Are you under pressure from other work? Have you any personal problems that he or she can help you to deal with?

Combining academic expectations with managerial requirements, Phillips and Pugh (1994: 148–154) list the following expectations students have of their supervisors:

- 'Students expect to be supervised';
- 'Students expect supervisors to read their work well in advance';
- 'Students expect their supervisors to be available when needed';
- 'Students expect their supervisors to be friendly, open and supportive';

- 'Students expect their supervisors to be constructively critical';
- 'Students expect their supervisors to have a good knowledge of the research area'.

While your supervisor has responsibilities towards you, he or she will also expect some obligations from you in return. According to Blaxter *et al.* (1996: 126), some duties expected by supervisors of their students are:

- to arrange regular meetings;
- to maintain a regular work pattern;
- to discuss progress and problems fully.

In addition, Phillips and Pugh (1994: 93–99) identify the following obligations of doctoral students, which are also relevant to undergraduate projects:

- 'to be independent';
- 'to produce written work that is not just a first draft';
- 'to be honest when reporting on their progress';
- to follow advice that is given;
- 'to be excited about their work'.

5.4.2 Using your supervisor effectively

The main contact you have with your project supervisor will be through pre-arranged meetings. These meetings may be at a regular time each week or more infrequent, perhaps only occurring every four or five weeks or more. As academic staff tend to be extremely busy, they are often difficult to find at other times and unlikely to be able to see you. You therefore need to make optimum use of the time you do see them during these meetings.

- Prepare for your meetings. Don't just turn up to a meeting with your supervisor without any ideas on what you want to get out of it. Think about what you want to discuss, decide what advice you want from your supervisor on which aspects of your project, and go prepared to present some of your own ideas and plans.
  Ricketts (1998: 17) suggests using the minutes of your previous meeting as a starting point for discussion each time. This helps to remind everyone of the current state of your project and identifies the work you were expecting to complete since the last meeting.
- As part of your meetings you may well want to discuss the following topics each time:
  - what progress you have made since the last meeting – work you have done, articles you have read, literature found, interviews conducted, programs developed, plans made, and so on.
  - what problems you have encountered – how you overcame them or whether you need help.

- who you have met – what did you discuss with them?
- what you intend to do next – is this suitable? Has your supervisor any other suggestions?

- Make notes during your meetings. It is unlikely that you will be able to remember everything that is discussed. Make notes as you go along and clarify things that you are not sure about before you leave. If you don't understand something that your supervisor is saying you must tell him or her. It is far better to get things clarified at an early stage than six months later when you realise you haven't investigated an important topic and perhaps omitted something vital from your project.
- Arrange your next meeting. It is usually a good idea to arrange the time and date of your next meeting before you leave. Agree some goals and targets with your supervisor that you intend to complete before your next meeting. This will give you something to work towards and will provide some motivation as you know your supervisor will be checking up on your progress at the next meeting.
- Follow your supervisor's advice. There is no point in going to meetings with your supervisor if you are going to ignore any advice given. Clearly, there are times when your supervisor will make *suggestions* that you might not want to follow. However, your supervisor will generally provide you with invaluable advice that you would be unwise not to take on board.

5.5 Working in teams

Due to increasing numbers of students within higher education, group working for projects and assignments is becoming more and more common. However, it is also recognised that group work has a number of educational and practical advantages for students, as Blaxter *et al.* (1996: 46) identify:

- It enables responsibility to be shared;
- You are able to specialise in areas you are comfortable with and good at;
- It provides experience of teamwork;
- You can perform much larger projects than you could achieve on your own;
- You have a 'support network' of colleagues.

Above all, working in teams will provide you with an invaluable experience in interacting with others, sharing work, overcoming joint difficulties and introducing you to the working practices of the 'real world'.

Many students resent working in teams as they feel their grades may be adversely affected by other people over whom they have no control. Others enjoy the experience and feel their team achieves far more than they could have done as individuals. Whatever the case, at one stage or another you may well find yourself conducting a computing project as part of a team on your course. This section discuss the issues involved in teamwork and presents some tips to help you complete team projects successfully.

5.5.1 Team roles

Whether you can choose your own team or whether your group is assigned to you at 'random', all your team members will bring two kinds of skills into your group: *personal* or *team skills* and *technical skills*. An imbalance within either of these skill areas in your group will probably lead to a poor team performance. Consequently, it is not always a good idea to form a group with your friends, who may all have similar interests, personalities and technical skills to you. If you can, take careful note of the following skill types and select a group with a good balance of these skills.

Belbin (1993) identifies nine personal or team skills:

- Plant: creative people with imagination who can solve difficult problems;
- Resource investigator: extrovert communicators – good for making contacts;
- Coordinator: good managers, delegators, chairperson;
- Shaper: dynamic people who thrive under pressure and overcome obstacles;
- Monitor/evaluator: see all options and maintain a strategic view of the project;
- Team worker: cooperative, diplomatic and good listeners;
- Implementer: disciplined, reliable, and efficient;
- Completer: conscientious, attend to detail well and finish work on time;
- Specialist: narrow specialism and viewpoint but dedicated.

Chances are that you will not be working in a team of this size. However, individuals within your team may well possess two or three of Belbin's team skill traits, giving your group a reasonable skills balance. Having a good cross-section of team skills within your group is, however, no guarantee of project success. Having said this, the more of these skills that are present within your group, the higher the chances are that the team will succeed. Individuals will work together well and the team will not suffer from clashes between the egos of several like-minded people.

These skill traits should be kept in mind when team roles are assigned. Three team roles that are common to all project teams, irrespective of the project, are:

- *Team leader*: chairperson, coordinator. The team leader is responsible

for timetabling the work, assigning it, chasing team members' progress, chairing meetings.
- *Librarian/secretary*: minutes meetings, coordinates paperwork and all literature.
- *Team contact*: liaises with external bodies – the client, supervisor etc.

When assigning these roles you might, for example, elect your team leader as the person possessing the skills of a *coordinator*. A *resource investigator* would perhaps be a good person to assign as your team contact, and the team's librarian/secretary may be best assigned to a *completer*.

Sometimes you may find that no one naturally fits into any of these roles or you may find that no one is willing to take on a particular role. In these cases the role might have to be divided so that different people are responsible for it or different people take on the role at different stages of the project. For example, team leadership could be split into coordinating team contributions, chairperson, planner etc. This is not an ideal solution as projects should ideally have a single leader, but it is a compromise.

Technical skills are particularly important within computing projects. Depending on the nature of your course, and the type of project you are undertaking, you will need team members with some of the following technical abilities:

- Programming – high level, low level, 4GLs, visual programming etc;
- Databases – analysis, design, development;
- Systems analysis;
- Systems design;
- Information systems;
- Human–computer interaction;
- Networking;
- Computer systems architecture;
- Graphics;
- Mathematics (including statistical analyses etc).

O'Sullivan *et al.* (1996) suggest using a SWOT analysis to identify team responsibilities. A SWOT analysis identifies everyone's Strengths, Weaknesses, Opportunities and Threats. For example, your own personal SWOT analysis might look something like this:

Strengths	*Weaknesses*
Strong leader	Relating to people I don't know
Technically sound	Writing skills
Good programmer	
Opportunities	*Threats*
Project is a chance to improve my systems analysis skills	Field trip clashes with project presentation

Not only must your team be well balanced with respect to technical skills and the team skills identified earlier, but your team must also *link* well. In other words, there must be good communication between team members in order for the project to succeed. This boils down to people's ability to get on with one another and is the main benefit of being in a group with your friends.

5.5.2 **Managing the team**

You have 'selected' your team and the project is under way – how should the group and its communications be managed? Group coordination will clearly rest on the shoulders of the team leader. It is his or her responsibility to co-ordinate effort by breaking a large project down into manageable chunks and assigning these chunks appropriately.

The main coordinating link that should be maintained within a group project is through frequent team meetings. These should be minuted, everyone should be in attendance, and work should be agreed and assigned. When work is assigned you should all agree on what should be done *and* by when. Work should be assigned to individuals based on their technical skills, and sometimes subgroups might form to work on particular parts of the project. The Gantt charts and activity networks introduced in Chapter 3 can help you assign work to team members, as they provide a strategic view of workloads and responsibilities. It is useful to get people to sign up to their obligations at this stage so that everyone knows who is responsible for what. If problems do arise later, and the team falls apart for whatever reason, individual contributions can be identified for assessment purposes.

Frequent meetings also provide a useful means of project control. They enable progress to be monitored and provide a time and place for team members to meet and discuss ideas. Motivation of team members also becomes clear at frequent meetings and any problems can perhaps be dealt with sooner rather than later.

5.5.3 **Teamwork tips**

- Have a single project manager/team leader. It is often tempting in group work to have a rather democratic, leader-less structure. However, somebody *does* need to be in charge of your project's management, he or she needs to coordinate the effort of everybody involved, keep a strategic view on your project's progress and make 'unpopular' decisions. If the group has two or three members who would like to lead the team then perhaps this could be achieved on a rotational basis. This could be managed by rotating the team leader based on each team member's technical contribution and effort, which will vary during the course of the project. Alternatively, as mentioned earlier, the team

leader's role could be divided among those wishing to lead the group but this is less satisfactory.
- Maintaining everyone's interest and motivation throughout the course of a large project can be difficult. For example, systems analysts would be busier at the earlier stages of a project than the end when, perhaps, programmers become overburdened. To overcome these problems try to plan into your project's schedule team responsibilities as well as technical activities. For example, the systems analyst might take over the group's secretarial/library activities as the project progresses, a programmer may relinquish the leader's role etc.
- In line with the points made above, it is important to ensure that people aren't overburdened with technical *and* team roles. It can take a lot of time to manage a group alongside other activities. You should ensure that team roles are accounted for when work is assigned to each member of your group. For example, a good team coordinator, who can motivate and coordinate everyone's contributions, may be assigned this task as his or her only role.
- Make sure that all meetings are fully documented and people 'sign up' to work commitments. Not only does this provide people with a 'contract' which they feel obliged to fulfil but, also, if things go wrong, arguments won't start over claims that 'X said they would do this' and 'Y promised that'.
- Maintain good communication between all team members. Make sure that a contact sheet for every team member is produced at the project's start with everybody's home address, telephone number and email address. Hold frequent short meetings, not long infrequent ones. Try to make full use of all the communication tools available to you. These can include facilities such as electronic diaries to plan meetings, and email to support team communication. Email can also be used to transfer documents and files between team members as attachments. Also try to set up shared directories on your institution's computer servers so that all team members have access to the latest project files (but ensure that some form of configuration management is in place).
- Try to create a team spirit. Create an identity with a team name and try to arrange some informal, social meetings as well as your formal ones.
- Try to maintain a single person to act as a liaison with external bodies such as your client, technical support staff, supervisor etc. Even if two or three of you attend client meetings it should be made clear who the contact person is within the group. This ensures that a consistent message is presented to external bodies and contradictions are avoided. It also avoids contradictory information passing into your group from two or three team members who may have approached the client on different occasions and received contradictory requests.

5.6 Summary

- All projects have five elements that require managing to some extent as the project progresses: *time*, *cost*, *quality*, *scope* and *resources*. These elements need to be balanced against one another so that you achieve your project's aims and objectives.
- Of these five elements, cost is something over which you probably have little concern or control. Quality and scope are the two elements you have most responsibility for and control over. Resources are those that are available to accomplish your project – you, your supervisor, your project team. The time you are allocated to complete your project cannot usually be extended so you need to employ time management techniques to manage this time more effectively.
- Time management consists of three stages: decide what you want to do, analyse what you are currently doing, and change the way you do things. There are only two ways to reduce the time you spend doing things: ditch them (perhaps by getting somebody else to do them – delegation) or use the time you have more effectively.
- Your supervisor is an invaluable resource. You will probably only see your supervisor at prearranged meetings so these must be planned for and used effectively.
- Working in teams brings a number of advantages and disadvantages. Each team member contributes two kinds of skill: team skills and technical skills. When work is assigned to team members try to balance team roles with technical duties and assign work and responsibilities according to people's strengths and weaknesses. Meet regularly and maintain good communication.

5.7 Further reading

Bliss, E.C. (1976) *Getting Things Done*, Futura, London.
Ferner, J.D. (1980) *Successful Time Management*, John Wiley and Sons, New York.
Garratt, S. (1985) *Manage Your Time*, Fontana/Collins, London.
Goodworth, C.T. (1984) *How You Can Do More in Less Time*, Business Books, London.
Haynes, M.E. (1987) *Make Every Minute Count*, Crisp Publications, Los Altos, California.
Turla, P. and Hawkins, K.L. (1985) *Time Management Made Easy*, Panther Books, London.

5.8 Exercises

1. Identify how the five project elements (resources, time, cost, quality, scope) relate to your own computing project. Which of these elements is your main focus/concern at the moment?
2. How could the student have managed his or her time more effectively in Table 5.1?
3. Put together a time log for yourself during the coming week.
4. Categorise your use of time into important/unimportant, urgent/non-urgent, and essential types. How can you reduce the time you spend on unimportant activities?
5. Plan for a meeting with your project supervisor.
6. If you are working on a group project try to identify which of Belbin's (1993) team skills each of your group possesses. Have you assigned roles based on these skills? Are technical tasks and team roles balanced logically and evenly among your team's members?

PART III

Presenting your project

CHAPTER 6
Presenting your project in written form

Aims
To introduce the skills needed to present your project effectively in written form.

Learning objectives
When you have completed this chapter, you should be able to:

- Understand how to structure and write professional reports;
- Write clear and concise abstracts;
- Understand how to present data and results clearly;
- Understand how to reference material and avoid plagiarism;
- Document software, comment programs and write user guides.

6.1 Introduction

In Chapter 1 dissemination of your ideas and results was identified as an important part of the research project process. Quite often a report is the only evidence of your project, unless you have developed a substantial piece of software. Although the report represents your project, remember that the good work you have performed can be ruined by a poor report. There is no point in performing a tremendous amount of valuable and important computing work, research and development if you cannot present your findings to other people. Conversely, a bad project cannot be turned into a good one by producing a good report. Although you can improve a poor project with a good report you must remember that your report is a reflection of your project and you *cannot* disguise sloppy investigation, development, implementation, analyses and method with a few carefully chosen words.

This chapter focuses on the presentation of written material for your project: structuring reports, writing abstracts, referencing material and presenting data. It also covers topics such as documenting software, commenting programs and writing user guides. How you present your project in oral form, through presentations and vivas, is the subject of the next chapter.

6.2 Writing and structuring reports

6.2.1 Considerations

There are two main considerations that you should bear in mind as you begin work on your project's report:

- Who is going to read it? What do they already know? What do you want them to learn? What do you want them to gain from your report? How do want to influence them?
- How long should it be? Has your institution set upper (and possibly lower) limits on the length of your report to which you must adhere? Based on the work you have performed and the findings you have obtained, what is a reasonable length for your report?

These considerations will influence what you decide to include and what you omit from your final report. You should not include material merely for the sake of it as this might irritate the reader and appear like 'padding'. Similarly, you should not leave material out of your report if you think it is important. Try to get the balance right – understand what it is you are trying to say, be aware of what the reader already knows, and include material appropriately.

6.2.2 Approaches to writing

There are two main approaches that people tend to use when they write reports: the *top-down approach* and the *evolutionary delivery*. These two approaches are not mutually exclusive and you may well find yourself adopting both of them to one extent or another as you develop your project's report.

The top-down approach is used to identify the structure of your report – how many chapters it will have, what each chapter will contain and how each chapter will break down into subsections. Using this approach will enable you to identify specific sections within each chapter as and when you know more about their content. With subheadings identified you can then go on to complete these sections, finishing them at an appropriate point in your project when results are obtained and information is acquired. Figure 6.1 provides an example breakdown for this particular chapter. By identifying the content of this chapter as a number of 'chunks' it makes writing much easier and less daunting as individual sections can be tackled one at a time. By identifying the overall structure of a chapter it also allows you to keep an eye on the overall target of that chapter so that you do not depart along tangents and discuss extraneous ideas that are out of context with the main point. Chapter

WRITING AND STRUCTURING REPORTS 111

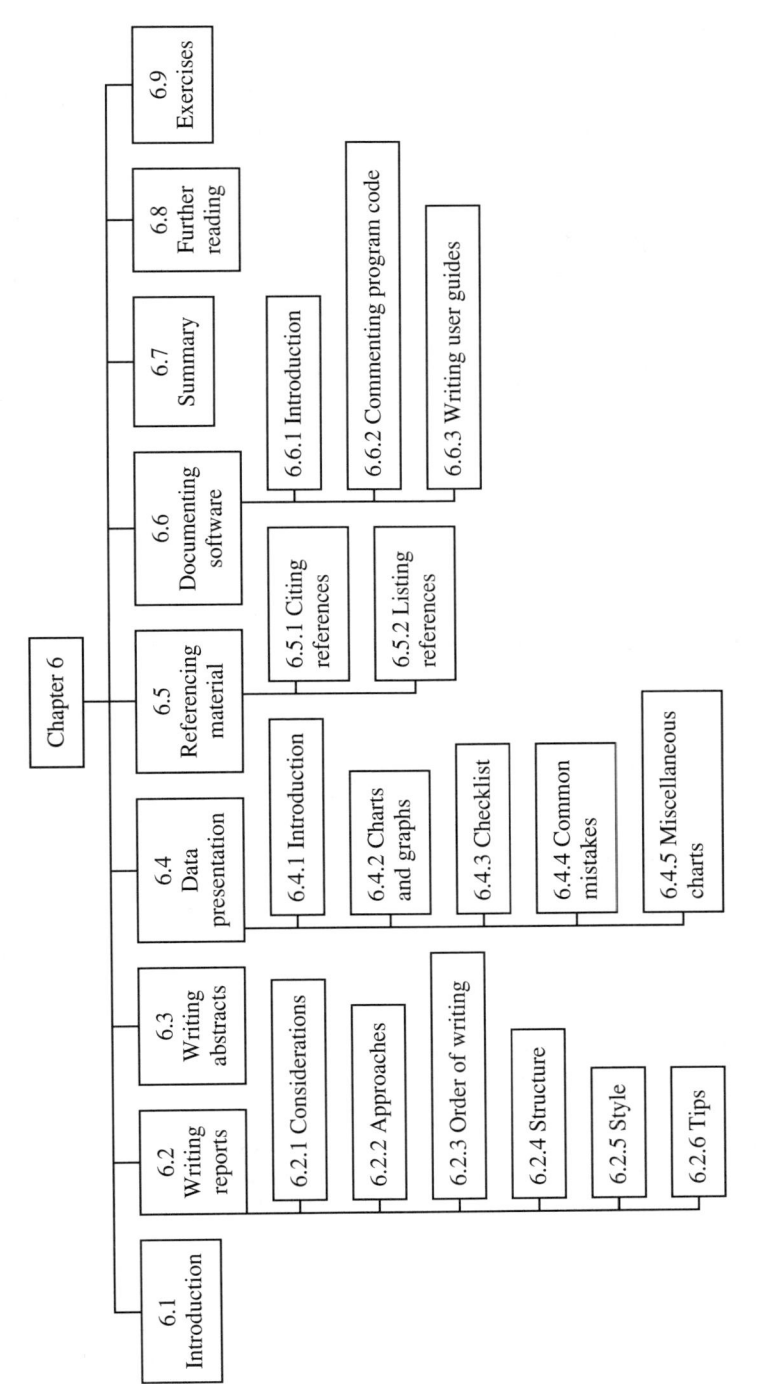

Figure 6.1 A chapter breakdown structure

breakdowns also help with time management in that they provide you with a better understanding of the amount of writing you have to do. This stems from an understanding of the complexity of each section, which will give you an idea of how long these sections will take to complete.

You might try to identify sections and subsections in your report very early on in your project. However, as is often the case, it is not until you finally come to complete your project that you fully understand what you want to include and can identify the specific content of every chapter. Whatever happens, you will find that a report breakdown structure is a useful way of structuring your thoughts and ideas and identifying how they will link together within the content of your report.

The other approach that is often used to write reports is the evolutionary delivery. Many people use this approach but are not conscious that they are doing so. In this approach you begin to write parts of your report and rewrite these parts as your project progresses. Each part thus evolves and matures over a period of time as new ideas emerge and your understanding increases. Thus, you do not sit down at the end of your project and write your report as a one-off. You write it over a much longer period of time during the lifetime of your project.

The two approaches introduced above can be combined so that you identify, perhaps at the start of your project, the specific sections of your report's chapters. You can then begin to write these sections but will find that they evolve and change as your project progresses. You might also find that your report breakdown structure itself evolves over time as your understanding increases, your ideas change and develop, and you obtain your results.

6.2.3 *The order of writing*

Whether you leave your final write-up until the end of your project or develop your report as your project progresses, there is a particular order of writing that you should try to follow. This order breaks down as follows:

- *Identify structure.* This relates to both the content of your report, using a report breakdown structure, and the formatting structure of your report in terms of font size and type, page size, numbering conventions and so on.

    Although a specific content structure might not be entirely clear to you at this stage, you should attempt to produce as much detail for each chapter's breakdown as possible. Report breakdown structures were discussed in the previous section.
- *Identify presentational style.* You should also try to set standards at this stage on the presentational aspects of your report – its layout. This will save time later when you are trying to collate your chapters and sections and find they are presented inconsistently. Make sure that you follow

any guidelines that your institution provides. If there are no guidelines, Cornford and Smithson (1996: 154) identify a number of points you should consider for your report's layout:

- avoid broad, open spaces or cramped layouts. Try to make sure figures and tables do not force large gaps into your text;
- use a clear 11 or 12 point font. Use something that is easy to read such as Times or Geneva;
- use a single, justified column with adequate margins for binding. However, it is sometimes argued that two columns are easier to read than one as text lines are shorter. Check your institution's guidelines and ask your supervisor for advice;
- use page numbers centred at the foot of each page.

You might also wish to define your own presentation style such as line spacing ($1\frac{1}{2}$ or double spaced), a section numbering convention (for example, '1.2 Section Title') and paragraph styles (for example, start each paragraph on a new line tabbed in eight spaces).

With the proliferation of colour printers these days, you might also wish to decide how to use colours to enhance text and presentation within your report. Be careful not to introduce a complex style such as red text for chapter titles, blue for section headings and so on. This kind of presentation looks very messy and it is best to stick with black text for the bulk of your report. Colours can, however, be used very effectively to enhance tables and highlight certain points. For example, to distinguish different parts of a table presenting statistical data, you might wish to use colour to highlight significant results.

- *Draft the introduction.* The introduction gives the reader an idea of the report's content so it should also help you to clarify your ideas. At this stage, however, your introduction will only be a first draft as your ideas are bound to evolve and your emphasis change by the time you have completed your report. Remember that your introduction might include, or consist mainly of, your literature review. As such, it should be tackled early so that your grounding in the subject is complete.
- *Main body.* The main body of your report is the next part you should work on. You might include chapters such as methods used, analyses performed and so on. Clearly, the content of the main body of your report will depend on the project you have undertaken. You may find that you write parts of the main body of your report as your project progresses and you will not necessarily write each chapter or section in order. You will find that different aspects of your project are completed at different times – not necessarily in the same order that you decided to present them in your report.
- *Conclusions and recommendations.* Quite clearly your conclusions and recommendations should be one of the last things that you complete.

Only when your project is complete will you fully understand what you have achieved and be able to present your final ideas and recommendations.
- *Complete the introduction.* As part of the evolutionary approach to writing you may well find that your introduction needs some reworking after you have completed the rest of your project's report. You may want to include some text alluding to your final results or introduce more background on a topic you have since focused on in more detail within your report.
- *Write the abstract.* You cannot really write a clear abstract for your report until you know what has been included in the report. How to write effective abstracts is covered in detail later in this chapter.
- *References and appendices.* Although you will be collating references and appendices as your project progresses, you should not complete their presentation until the rest of the report has been written. References may be added or deleted and you may decide to include or exclude material from the appendices.
- *Arrange contents list and index.* Leave the completion of an index (if one is required) and your contents list until the end. Only then will you know the exact content of your report and all page numbers.
- *Proofread, check and correct.* It is vitally important to proofread your report after it is completed. Quite often, because you have been so close to your report for so long, reading through your report straight away might mean that you miss glaring errors or omissions. You know what you meant to write so this is what you read, whether it is written or not. With this in mind it is a good idea to leave your report for a day or two before proofreading it or, preferably, get someone else to do it for you. Bear in mind that if you do this you will need to complete your report a few days before its deadline to allow yourself time for proofreading and correcting or changing any points that emerge.

6.2.4 **Structure**

Your report should be structured into the following sections:

- Title page. Follow any guidelines provided. As a minimum you should include: title, author, date and degree award.
- Abstract.
- Acknowledgements to people you wish to thank for helping you with your project.
- Contents listing.
- List of figures and tables. This is not compulsory and you should include these lists only if you feel they will add value to your report and will be useful for the reader.

- The report itself:
    - Introduction/literature review. The first chapter of your report should always be an introduction. Quite often introductory chapters serve to present the literature review. Alternatively, the introduction serves as a brief overview of the project and the report, and the literature review is presented as a chapter in its own right later. Your introduction should set the scene for the project report, and should include your project's aims and purpose.
    - Main body.
    - Conclusions/recommendations.
- References, presented in an appropriate format. Referencing material is discussed in more detail later.
- Appendices, labelled as Appendix A, Appendix B, Appendix C etc. These may include program listings, test results and project details such as your initial proposal, your project plan and meeting reports.
- Glossary of terms, if required.
- Index, if required, but avoid if possible.

6.2.5 Style

The style of writing that you adopt to present your report can be discussed from three points of view. First is the actual presentation style of your report – for example, its layout, font and so on. This kind of style was discussed earlier. Second is the style of grammar that you use within your report. Quite often good reports can be ruined by poor grammar. The author's meaning is unclear as ideas and results are hidden within long complex sentences that include excessive words and jargon. The third point of view is overall content structure, which will be discussed later.

A good writing style comes with practice – the more that you write, the clearer and easier it becomes. Reading also helps to improve your own writing skills as you learn elements of good practice and identify interesting ways of discussing and presenting arguments. Having said this, there are some simple rules that anyone can follow to improve their writing style for professional reports. Try to avoid using personal pronouns such as I, you, we, my and so on, but make sure that you don't end up producing elaborate, complex sentences just to avoid this. Your supervisor should be able to advise you here and it may be that the nature of your project requires you to use the personal approach. Keep sentences short and to the point. Avoid making several points within the same sentence. Avoid abbreviations, jargon and slang. Use simple rather than complex words; the latter are often irritating for the reader, cloud the meaning of your sentence and are often used to hide your own lack of understanding about the subject, which the educated reader will spot.

It is common practice to present your report in the past tense as the report represents the results of the project which you *have* completed. Having said this, Day (1995) suggests that the present tense should be used when referring to the work of others (just like this sentence does!). Avoid jokes and personal asides. Avoid shortened forms such as 'isn't' instead of 'is not'. Make sure you know how to use apostrophes – for example, 'John's computer' rather than 'Johns computer'. Finally, make sure that you use a spell checker; sloppy spelling puts many reports into a bad light.

Moving away from basic grammar, the third style to consider when writing project reports is overall content structure. Your report should be constructed so that it has:

- *a beginning:* the introduction and literature review which set the scene;
- *a middle:* the bulk of your report where the main component of your project is discussed;
- *an end:* conclusions, summary, recommendations and future work.

This kind of structure should also be evident within individual chapters of your report. They too should have an introduction (possibly a chapter overview), the main body of the chapter and an end (possibly a chapter summary or conclusions from the chapter).

6.2.6 **Tips**

This section on report writing is concluded by presenting a few tips to help you. Bell (1993: 152) identifies a number of points that can help you discipline yourself and improve your writing skills.

- Set deadlines. Your report will take a long time to produce. If you do not set yourself deadlines and stick to them you will not finish on time. Using a report breakdown structure can help you to plan your time commitments to your report.
- Write regularly. Find your best time of day for writing and your favourite location. In other words, make sure that you 'write when your mind is fresh' and 'find a regular writing place' (Saunders *et al.* 1997: 371). People often find they cannot write with distractions or when they are over-tired.
- Create a work rhythm. Once you are under way, keep going. Don't stop to check a reference if the text is flowing, keep going until you reach a natural break.
- Write up sections when they are ready – when they are clear in your mind. This will also save time towards the end of your project when your project write-up might be little more than a collation of your existing text and producing an introduction and conclusion.
- Stop at a point from which it is easy to restart. It can often take a lot of time to get going again after a break so try to stop at a natural break in

your report; for example, when you have completed an entire section. Trying to pick up from where you left off the previous day or week can be difficult as you might have forgotten what it was you intended to write. If a break in your work is unavoidable, make a note of what you intended to do next so that when you come back to your writing later you can pick up from where you left off more easily.

Another tip worth following is to collate all the material you will need together before starting to write. Breaking your writing flow to search for a reference or visit the library to trace a vital book will not help.

For computing students it almost goes without saying that the best way to produce your report is with a word processor of one kind or another. These packages are far more effective than typewritten or handwritten work alone. Almost all word processors these days come with dictionaries and thesaurus facilities built in. In addition, many are equipped with equation editors that can help you produce neat equations embedded within your text. Alternatively, equation editors are available that can be used to 'construct' equations before pasting them into your report. The following is an example of an equation that has been pasted into the text. Notice how this equation has been given a reference number (6.1 in this case), which you should always include to uniquely identify each equation you incorporate in your report.

$$f(N) = \frac{\Sigma N(N-1)}{\sqrt{S^2(N-1)}} \qquad (6.1)$$

Be careful when using in-built spell checkers. Many are based on US English dictionaries and will change words to the US English equivalent; for example 'center' instead of 'centre'. Spell checkers might also change spelling 'errors' within verbatim quotes you have used from other authors.

Grammar checkers should also be used with caution. What might appear an elegant, well-constructed sentence to you, might be changed automatically by a grammar checker. However, if you feel that your grammar is weak, these facilities are invaluable.

6.3 Writing abstracts

Blaxter *et al.* (1996: 238) define the function of an abstract as to 'summarize briefly the nature of your research project, its context, how it was carried out, and what its major findings are'. The abstract provides the reader with an overview of your project and is the basis on which many readers will decide whether or not to read your report at all. With this in mind your abstract should be concise (preferably no more than one page long), clear and interesting.

Many abstracts are structured like a contents listing, but this is of little value

118 PRESENTING YOUR PROJECT IN WRITTEN FORM

to the reader, who can refer to the report's actual contents list for this kind of information. Your report's abstract should be one of the last things you write, when you actually know what you have achieved and what the content of your report is. Avoid using references in your abstract as the reader will not necessarily wish to search through your report to find them or be familiar with the author(s) you have cited. In addition, avoid using jargon and acronyms – these should be introduced only in the main body of your report. Writing good abstracts is something that comes with practice. To get a 'feel' for good and bad abstract presentation pay careful attention to the way others structure the abstracts of articles that you obtain.

Take, as examples, the following abstracts for the same article, based on an artificial neural network approach to predicting software development costs.

Abstract 1

This article investigates the application of ANNs to software development cost estimation. It begins by discussing existing software prediction techniques such as COCOMO (Boehm 1981) and Delphi (Helmer-Heidelberg 1966). The article identifies the process of software cost estimation and uses this as a basis on which to apply the ANNs developed for this project. Equations are presented showing how improvements can be made to the backpropagation algorithm used in ANN training. ANN simulation is also discussed. An evaluation of the results from the ANNs is presented and these results compare favourably with existing techniques identified in the paper.

Abstract 2

One of the major problems with software development projects is that it is extremely difficult to estimate accurately their likely cost, duration and effort requirements. This invariably leads to problems in project management and control. Part of the problem is that during the early stages of these projects very little is known about the problem domain and, consequently, initial estimates tend to be best guesses by a project manager. Artificial neural networks appear well suited to problems of this nature as they can be trained to understand the explicit and inexplicit factors that drive a software project's cost. For this reason, artificial neural networks were investigated as a potential tool to improve software project effort estimation using project data supplied by a software development company. In order to deal with uncertainties that exist in initial project estimates, the concept of neural network simulation was developed and

> employed. This paper discusses this concept and comments on the results that were obtained when artificial neural networks were trained and tested on the data supplied.

The first abstract is presented incorrectly, as a contents listing, while the second sets the scene for the article and identifies the content and contribution that the article is making. The first abstract is presented as a breakdown of the article's sections and it includes acronyms and references to papers that may be unfamiliar to the reader. When writing your own abstract try to follow the structure and style of the second abstract presented here.

6.4 Data presentation

6.4.1 *Introduction*

In almost all projects you will have to present data in one format or another – data you obtain from questionnaires or surveys, software test results, algorithm speed trials and so on. While textual presentation of numeric results can often provide a rather 'dry' interpretation of the information gathered, pictures, in the form of graphs and charts, provide a far more pleasing, holistic idea of what is going on. 'A diagram can often simplify quite complex data which could take a paragraph or more to explain' (Bell 1993: 147).

Although a picture is worth a thousand words you must ensure that the picture you are painting is the correct one and you are not presenting results in such a way as to hide their true meaning. According to Mark Twain, Benjamin Disraeli (1804–1881) said that there are three kinds of lies: 'lies, damned lies and statistics', the implication being that you can make statistical results say practically anything you want them to say. Remember, when you compile your report, that you must be objective and present your results in a clear and honest way. This section deals with presenting information using charts and tables, presenting various examples of some of the most popular charts that are used, and showing some instances where charts are used incorrectly.

6.4.2 *Presenting charts and graphs*

All figures and tables that you include within your report should be clearly and uniquely labelled with a number and a short description. The most common approach is to label each figure and table using consecutive numbers prefixed by the current chapter number. The approach used within this book, where we have, for example, 'Figure 6.1 *A chapter breakdown structure*', is quite a common standard which you can follow. Note that it is permissible to label a table and a figure with the same number; for example, Table 6.1 and Figure 6.1 refer to two different items within a report. Above all, be consistent and don't change the way in which figures and tables are labelled from one chapter to the next.

When you use figures and tables within a report they should be included because they add something of value to the report. They should not be included because you think they look nice. Figures and tables should help to clarify and support information you are presenting within the text of the report and should be included as close to their original reference point as possible, but not before. Take, as an example, Table 6.1. This table presents the final degree classifications of 100 students who completed their Computer Studies course in 1998.

Table 6.1 *Degree classification of 100 students*

1st	2:1	2:2	3rd	Pass	Fail
7	23	38	17	10	5

Table 6.1 presents these data in a much clearer way than you could hope to achieve using text alone. For example, compare this table with:

Seven students obtained first class degrees, twenty three obtained a 2 : 1, thirty eight achieved a 2 : 2, seventeen received 3rd class degrees, ten achieved only a Pass degree, and five students failed.

Although Table 6.1 is easier to follow than the text presented above, it is not necessarily the best way of presenting these data. Figure 6.2 is perhaps a clearer way of interpreting these results and it provides a more 'holistic' view of the spread, pattern or *distribution* of degree grades. Note that the distribution of data is only relevant when the data are of at least ordinal scaling. In other words, the categories into which the data are arranged represent an increasing magnitude of one kind of another (for example, the position of runners in a race; good, average or poor software quality and so on). Data that merely represent classes in which the order is irrelevant (for example, gender, religious belief and so on) have no distribution as such and the order of the columns in these charts is unimportant. In this case the chart can only emphasise the difference between the number of items identified within each category.

Figure 6.2 is a *vertical bar chart* or *column chart*. These charts can also be presented horizontally but, generally, the vertical representation is preferred. Bar charts are used to present categorial data and are useful for presenting the results of questionnaires that have used Likert-type scales. These scales indicate 'strength of agreement or disagreement with a given statement' (Bell 1993: 139); for example, 'Do you think this software is poor, average, or good?'. Note how, on this chart, the data have been split into columns with gaps in between, both axes have been labelled and the chart has been uniquely titled as Figure 6.2 with a corresponding brief label.

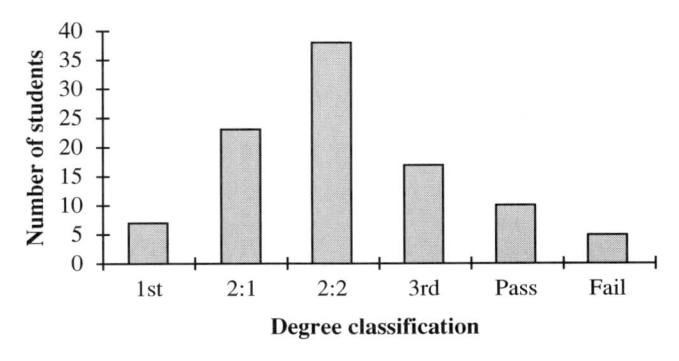

Figure 6.2 *Bar chart showing degree classification of 100 students*

For continuous data an alternative to the bar chart is required as the data are not arranged in distinct categories but can take any *real* value (for example, age, size, weight and so on). In these cases a *histogram* is used. Histograms present data in a similar way to bar charts in that columns are used to represent frequencies of occurrence of a particular data item. However, because histograms present continuous data, it is now up to you how you split the data into unique categories. Remember that bar charts have their categories defined for them based on the categories defined within the data they represent. As an example, Figure 6.3 presents a histogram showing the *age* of the 100 computer studies students.

In Figure 6.3 the age of graduates has been split into ten unique categories: 18 to 20, 20 to 22, 22 to 24, 24 to 26 years old etc. It has been assumed, in this case, that each category's upper boundary is actually one day before the year

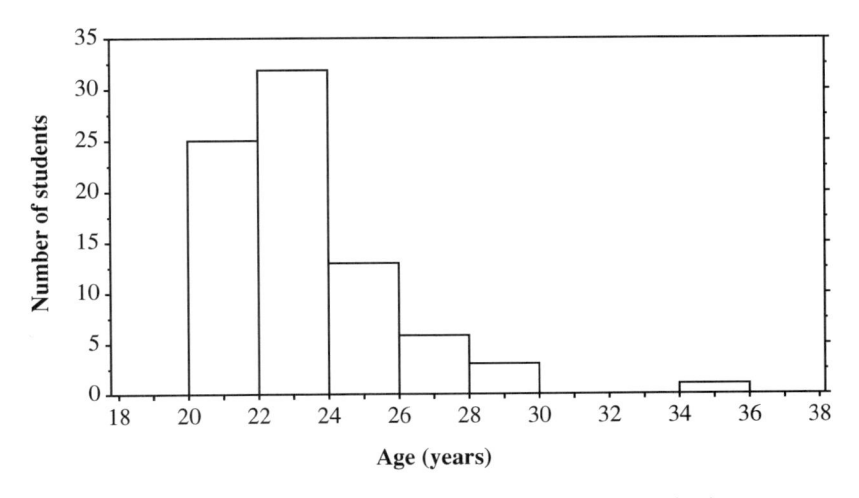

Figure 6.3 *Histogram showing age of 100 students at graduation*

122 PRESENTING YOUR PROJECT IN WRITTEN FORM

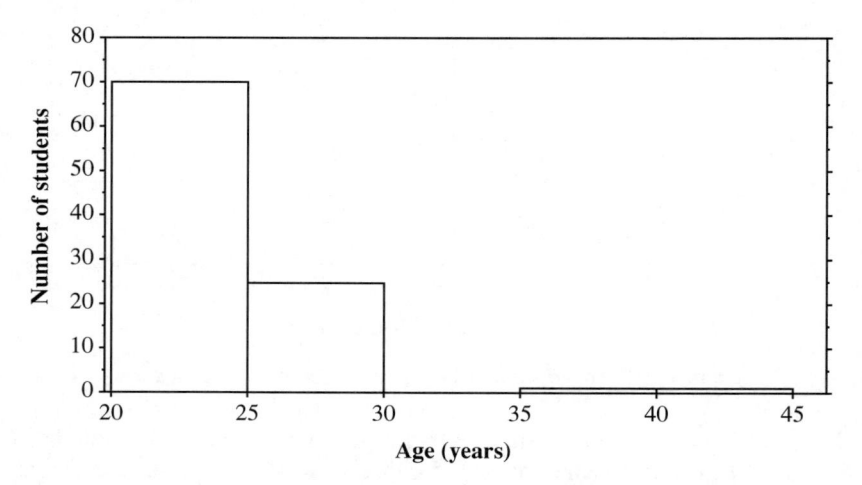

Figure 6.4 *Histogram showing age of 100 students at graduation*

indicated, so that people whose even birthday falls on the day of the survey will be placed in the next category up (that is, 20 to 22 actually represents 20 years to 21 years 364 days old). Each column now represents the number of students who fall within the defined range. Notice how the bars in this chart are now touching. This highlights the fact that the data are continuous and there is no absolute break between the categories.

There is no reason why you could not, alternatively, have defined the categories as 20 to 25, 25 to 30, 30 to 35 and so on. This results in the histogram shown in Figure 6.4.

Figure 6.4 provides a 'coarser' interpretation of the findings and, perhaps, provides a poorer overview of the spread of student ages at graduation. This figure emphasises the importance of carefully selecting appropriate categories for presenting continuous data in histograms. Splitting your data into too many categories can lead to a number of gaps, while splitting your data into too few categories can lead to broad, 'high' bars that provide little indication of the underlying distribution.

Another form of chart you may wish to use within your report is a *pie chart*. Pie charts are used to show *proportions* of categories within your data. Take, as an example, Figure 6.5, which presents the same data as those presented in Figure 6.2. While Figure 6.2 shows the distribution of actual marks, the pie chart in Figure 6.5 shows the proportion of students with particular degree classifications. Which figure you use would depend on what you were trying to emphasise or explain within your report. You would use a pie chart to discuss proportions and a bar chart to discuss distributions.

Pie charts come in various shapes and sizes – three-dimensional, exploded, coloured, shaded, wheels and so on – and most spreadsheet packages provide you with these formats. How you present your charts is clearly up to you, but

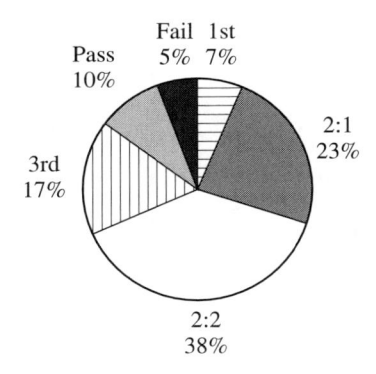

Figure 6.5 *Pie chart showing degree classification of 100 students*

don't get so carried away with a chart's presentation that you obscure the real meaning of the data you are presenting.

While you could use several pie charts next to one another to compare proportions between two or more subjects, a combined bar chart, such as that shown in Figure 6.6, can be used to present this comparison more clearly. In this case the spread of degree grades at four universities is presented. Notice how a legend has been included in this chart to identify the shading used in the columns, and how this legend and shading follows a logical top-down approach based on grades from 1st to Fail.

If you weren't interested in looking at proportions between categories but actual values, you could use a combined bar chart such as that shown in Figure 6.7. In this figure you can see the number of students graduating in Computer Studies categorised according to their gender. The bars are arranged in degree classification order and split according to gender. In this case gender is identified within each degree classification.

Note that the bar chart in Figure 6.7 has been presented in a rather conventional format. These days you will quite often see three-dimensional plots,

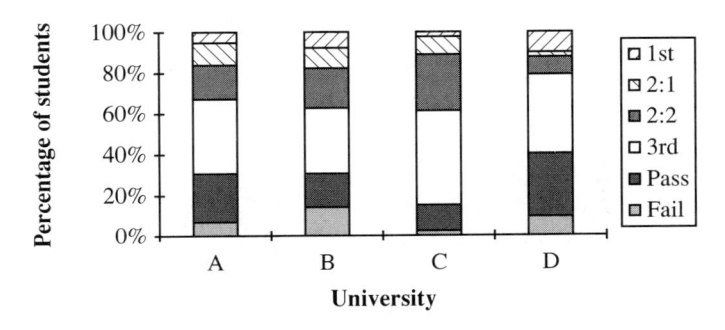

Figure 6.6 *Comparison of pass rates at four universities*

124 PRESENTING YOUR PROJECT IN WRITTEN FORM

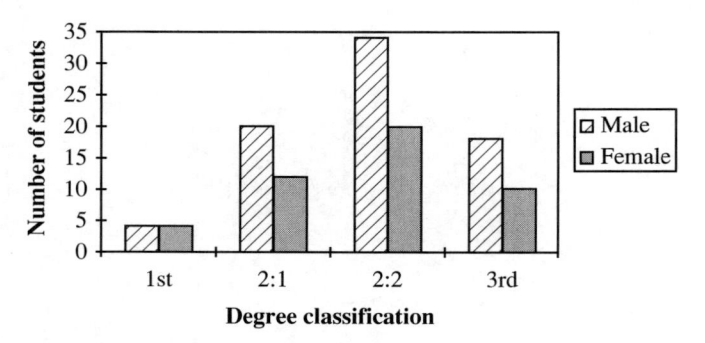

Figure 6.7 *Degree classification and gender of 125 recent graduates*

colours and shading used to enhance the attractiveness of such charts. Beware, however, as mentioned before, that you do not obscure the true meaning of what you are trying to portray or hide insignificant findings behind elaborate diagrams and figures.

Figure 6.8 takes the data used in Figure 6.7 and rearranges the groupings, thus presenting the results of Figure 6.7 in a slightly different way. This time the bars have been split into degree classifications and these grades grouped by gender. Once again, how you present these data is up to you and will depend on what you are trying to emphasise. Figure 6.7 is concerned with showing how each individual grade is spread between men and women. Figure 6.8 is concerned with showing the spread of grades for all men and the spread of grades for all women.

One drawback within Figures 6.7 and 6.8 is that the total numbers of male and female students differ. Ideally one would like to see the proportion of men obtaining Firsts, 2 : 1s, 2 : 2s etc. and be able to compare this with the proportion of women obtaining these grades. For example, do women, on average, obtain more first class degrees than men? Although you would need to perform a statistical analysis on your data to 'prove' this, the charts would present a clear, visual overview of the situation. Your *y*-axis in both of these cases would

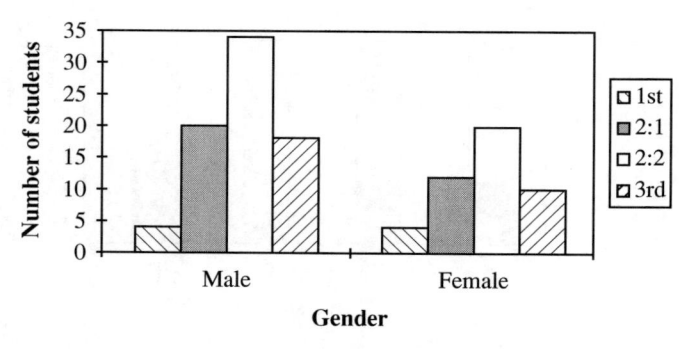

Figure 6.8 *Alternative view of degree classification and gender of 125 recent graduates*

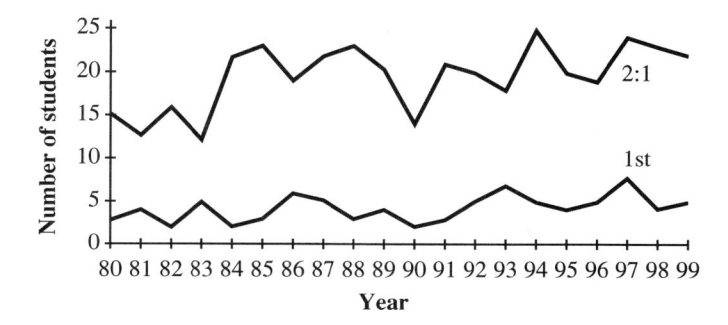

Figure 6.9 *Trends in first class and 2 : 1 degrees, 1980–1999*

be relabelled as 'Percentage of students' as opposed to 'Number of students' and the charts would provide a better comparison of grade spread based on gender – if this is what you wanted.

Another form of chart you may find useful is a *line chart*. These figures are generally used to show trends over periods of time. Figure 6.9 presents such a chart, in this case showing the trend (if indeed there is one) of first class and 2 : 1 degrees awarded between 1980 and 1999. Note that this only provides a visual interpretation of these data. You would need to perform some statistical analyses on your data to determine whether there was actually a significant trend or not. Statistical tests are beyond the intended scope of this book as there are numerous texts available that deal with these issues.

The last form of 'popular' chart to look at within this section is the *scatter diagram*. Scatter diagrams are used to show the relationship between two variables. For example, Figure 6.10 plots the assignment grades of 30 computing students against the number of hours each student worked on their assignment. Notice how the chart shows a general upward trend, perhaps indicating that there is a relationship between these two variables. Although the strength and significance of this relationship would be calculated statistically, the chart

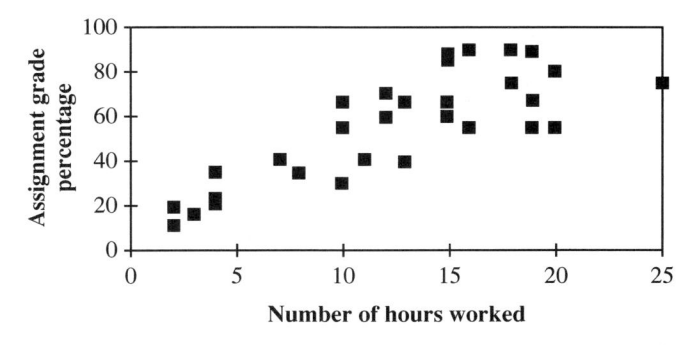

Figure 6.10 *Relationship between assignment grade and hours of effort of 30 students*

provides a visual interpretation of this relationship which is perhaps easier to follow than some statistical calculations. This is not to say that you could omit any rigorous statistical interpretation of data that you obtain but that you can support these calculations and improve their presentation by use of *appropriate* figures and tables within your report.

6.4.3 **Checklist**

Saunders *et al.* (1997: 299) present a checklist of points that you should observe when you have completed tables and figures within your report. For both diagrams and tables they recommend that you should ask yourself the following questions:

- Does it have a brief but clear and descriptive title?
- Are the units of measurement clearly stated?
- Are the sources of data used clearly stated?
- Are there notes to explain any abbreviations?
- Have you stated the sample size?

For diagrams the following checklist of questions is suggested:

- Does it have clear axis labels?
- Are bars and their components in the same logical sequence?
- Is more dense shading used for smaller areas?
- Is a key or legend included (where necessary)?

and for tables:

- Does it have clear column and row headings?
- Are columns and rows in a logical sequence?

6.4.4 **Common mistakes**

You should not include figures and tables within your report just for the sake of it. They should be there to support arguments you make within the text and to clarify, in diagrammatical form, data, results and interpretations you are making. This leads to the first common mistake that people sometimes make in using figures and tables – including them unnecessarily. Figure 6.11 is an example of just such a case where a pie chart is presented (sometimes even on a whole page) adding no value to the report whatsoever. In this case, as 100% of those questioned responded 'Yes', the use of the pie chart, which normally shows proportions, is unnecessary and makes the report look as though it is being padded out because it has little of real value to say.

The second common mistake made when using charts is to use them inappropriately when other charts would present your data in a much clearer light. Figure 6.12 provides just such an example – in this case a line chart is being

DATA PRESENTATION 127

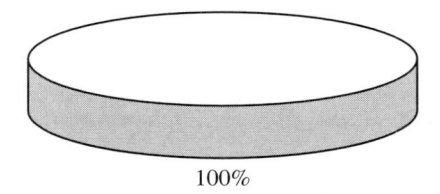

Figure 6.11 *100% of respondents said 'yes'*

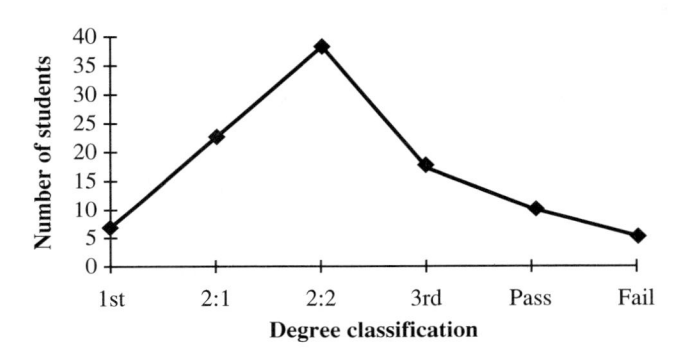

Figure 6.12 *'Incorrect' use of a line chart*

used when a trend is not the focus of attention. Although one might be interested in trying to identify the shape of the underlying distribution of degree grades, a bar chart would be more appropriate in this case.

Another common mistake people tend to make when including charts within reports is to scale them incorrectly. Sometimes this is done deliberately to hide the true meaning of the data that are presented. At other times it is done by accident when you are unsure about what your data are trying to tell you or what your data mean.

Figures 6.13 and 6.14 present a university department's spending between 1980 and 1999. Although both these figures present exactly the same data, using exactly the same type of chart, they appear very differently. Figure 6.13 shows, perhaps, an alarming decrease in spending during this period, while Figure 6.14 puts this 'trend' into perspective and shows that spending has changed only very slightly over this period of time. However, Figure 6.13 provides a good view of the *detail* of the spending changes while Figure 6.14 provides little information on what has happened. In Figure 6.14, it appears, unless you look very closely, that spending has not changed at all throughout this period, but you know this is not the case. These two figures emphasise the importance of getting scales right. You need to decide what it is you are attempting to show, not what you are attempting to hide, and scale your charts accordingly.

128 PRESENTING YOUR PROJECT IN WRITTEN FORM

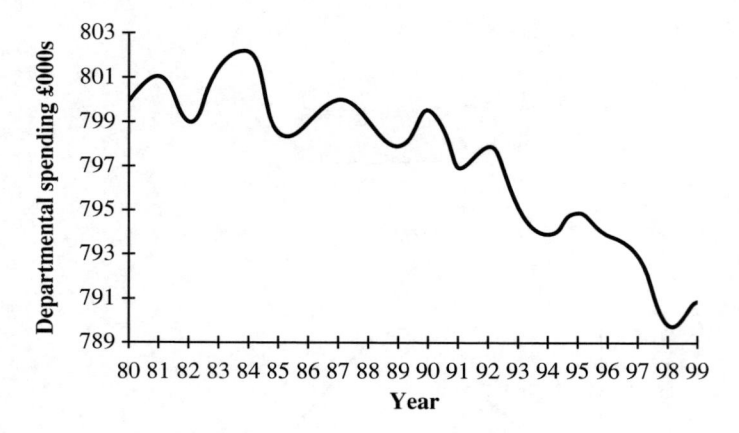

Figure 6.13 *'Dramatic' decline in spending*

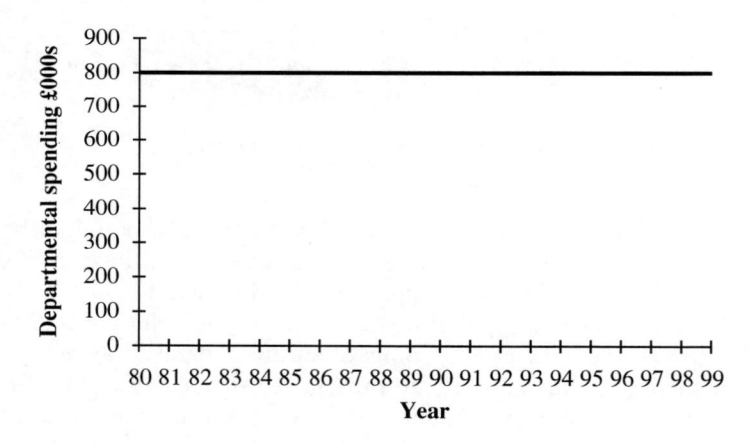

Figure 6.14 *Less dramatic decline in spending*

6.4.5 **Miscellaneous charts**

Some less common charts that you might come across and wish to use are presented in Figures 6.15–6.18. Figure 6.15 is a three-dimensional bar chart, which is used to enhance the appearance of 'bland' two-dimensional bar charts. While these charts don't necessarily add anything significant to the presentation of the data, they do provide a more visually appealing diagram.

Figure 6.16 is a *polar* chart, which is used to compare variables with several comparable factors. For example, each 'arm' of the polar chart would represent a particular factor and each shape would represent the variable in which you were interested. Each shape would thus provide an indication of the similarities

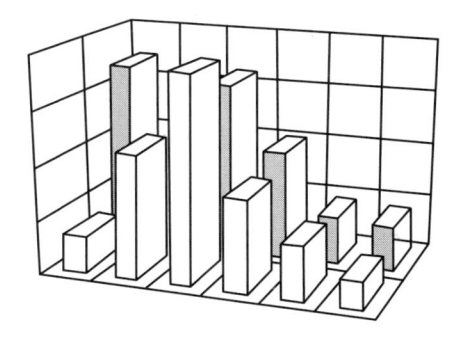

Figure 6.15 *An example three-dimensional bar chart*

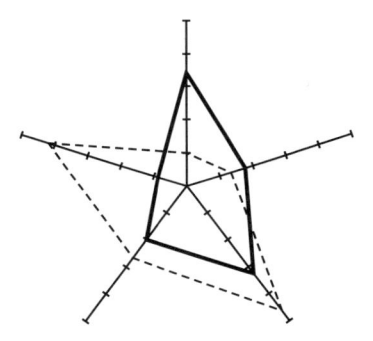

Figure 6.16 *An example polar chart*

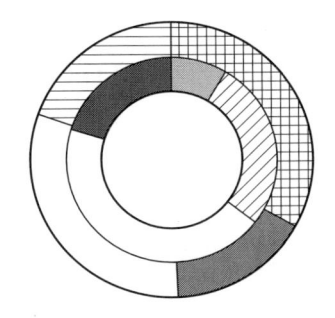

Figure 6.17 *An example doughnut chart*

and differences of each variable for each of the factors presented on each axis.

Figure 6.17 is a *doughnut* chart, which is another way of presenting a pie chart. The advantage of this representation is that you can now plot several pie charts together on the same figure to enable proportional comparisons between variables to be made.

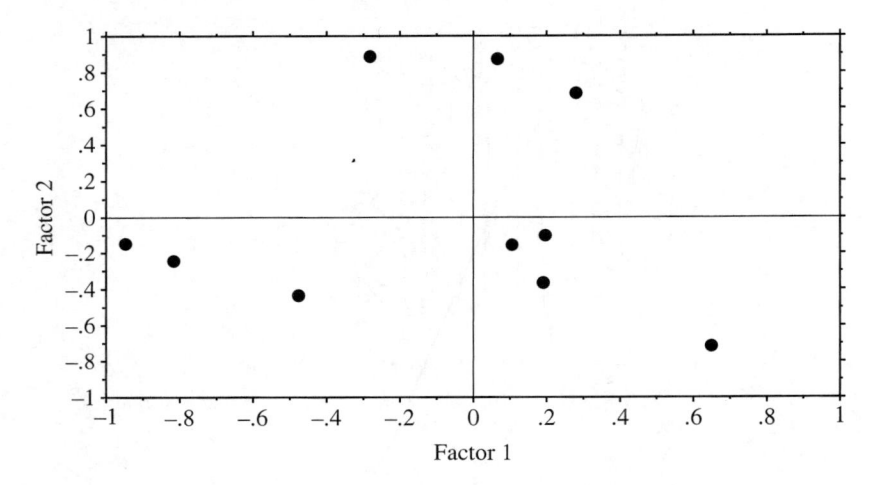

Figure 6.18 *An example factor analysis plot*

Figure 6.18 is a factor analysis plot, which presents the results of two combined factors from a factor analysis. This figure helps to show how variables are grouped together depending on a number of factors in two dimensions. While some of the variables may appear closely related to one another in this diagram, looking at other factors in other dimensions might show that they are not. Factor analysis is a statistical technique that can only really be performed using a computer and a statistical package. The calculations are much too complex to be performed by hand.

6.5 Referencing material and avoiding plagiarism

> Nothing is said that has not been said before.
> Terence (c. 195–159 BC), *The Eunuch*, Prologue

With Terence's statement in mind it is important that you support the work you are presenting within your report by appropriate references. Much of what you present will have been touched on, discussed, written about or covered by other authors in the past – particularly for undergraduate projects. Thus, any arguments that you make within your report and especially within your literature review should be justified 'by referencing previous research' (Saunders *et al.* 1997: 39). Material is referenced within reports to:

- *Avoid plagiarism.* In other words, you do not present other people's ideas, thoughts, words, figures, diagrams, results and so on without referencing them, in order to make their work look as if it is your own. Plagiarism can be performed accidentally or deliberately but in both

cases it is deemed a serious academic offence. This is one reason why you should perform an extensive literature survey – to ensure that you are not merely repeating the work of others.
- *Identify context*, to place your work in context with other recognised publications. This will strengthen your report by demonstrating how it builds and extends the work of others and showing how your work resides within a recognised academic field of study.
- *Support and validate*. Support your own arguments and validate any statements that you make. If you are making certain claims you will have to support these with either research results or references to other authors.
- *Identify sources*. Provide people reading your report with a comprehensive list of related work that they can use to study your topic in more detail or take your work further. By identifying sources clearly, people reading your report will be able to locate the articles you have used.

There are two aspects to referencing. The first aspect to consider is how to use references correctly within the body of your report – in terms of their presentation and appropriateness – called *citing*. The second aspect is how to present these references correctly at the end of your report. Each of these aspects will be dealt with in turn.

6.5.1 Citing references

Generally speaking, there are two ways to cite references, the *Harvard system* and the *numeric system* (also called the *Vancouver system*). Harvard is the better system to use as the numeric system requires each reference to be identified by a unique number, which needs updating every time you decide to add or remove a reference from your report. Quite often the numeric system also gives no indication of the author to whom you are referring and the reader has to search through the reference list at the back of your report to find this information.

These days, many word processing packages have reference management systems that enable you to maintain and update references within your report quickly and easily. In Chapter 4 a number of software tools were listed that can help you manage your references. However, with or without such a system, it is recommended that you use the Harvard style of referencing, which is more flexible and clearer than the numeric approach.

The Harvard system uses the name of the author(s) and the year of their publication to identify each reference uniquely within a report. For example, consider the following extracts from an undergraduate project report:

It is often said that computing is an art not a science (Smith and Jones 1993: 20) and

> It is often said that computing is an art not a science. This was first suggested by Smith and Jones (1993: 20) who justified their proposition by ...

The article by Smith and Jones is identified by its year of publication. If you are referring to more than one of their publications of the same year you would append letters to the date (a, b, c etc.) to uniquely identify each article – thus (Smith and Jones 1993a), (Smith and Jones 1993b) etc. The page number (20), where the point in question was made, has also been identified. This is common when referencing books, which obviously have many pages, but not when referencing journal articles.

An alternative way of presenting this argument, supported by the same reference, could be:

> Smith and Jones (1993: 20) state that 'computing has much more in common with the finer things in life, like art, than science or engineering'

In the previous examples the ideas of Smith and Jones had been put into our own words so quotation marks were unnecessary. However, because their text has now been used verbatim, this text *must* be included within quotation marks to show that these are their words, not ours. If you are quoting a large block of text it is acceptable to present that text without quotation marks providing it stands out from your own text in some way. For example, you would either present that text in italics, in a different font to the one you were using for your main text, or as a justified block of text between wider margins in your report.

According to Cornford and Smithson (1996: 142) there are only three occasions when you should quote other people's work verbatim:

- where the original author has presented something 'more succinctly, elegantly or clearly' than you could;
- 'where you need to prove that it was a particular author who wrote the words, or you are introducing some text in order to analyze it';
- where there is no way of paraphrasing; for example quoting lists.

You should also bear in mind that including too many direct quotations and references to other authors may *give away some authority* from your own work. In other words, you might include so much material from other authors that it is difficult for the reader to identify your contribution as much of the material presented is really the work of others.

Many articles are written by individuals. The Harvard system caters for single authors like this:

> It is often said that computing is an art not a science (Johnson 1992)

However, when there are more than two authors involved with the same article you generally omit all but the first author's name and use *et al.* instead:

It is often said that computing is an art not a science (Peterson *et al.* 1995)

When you wish to refer to more than one reference to support the arguments you are making in your report you would include them alphabetically:

It is often said that computing is an art not a science (Johnson 1992; Peterson *et al.* 1995; Smith and Jones 1993: 20)

Sometimes you will want to present a reference to an article you haven't read (a *secondary* reference) which has been cited by another author. In this case you only need to list the article you've read (the *primary* reference) and you should cite the reference like this:

It is often said that computing is an art not a science (Johnson 1992, cited by Markos *et al.* 1996)

Looking briefly at the numerical referencing format for completeness, in this case each reference is identified by a unique number:

It is often said that computing is an art not a science [1, 2].

Or:

It is often said that computing is an art not a science.[1,2]

Or:

Smith and Jones [2] state that 'computing has much more in common with the finer things in life, like art, than science or engineering'

In this case, each time a new reference is used within your report it is given a new reference number. References are then listed at the back of your report in numerical, rather than alphabetical, order. Notice that, if you decide to remove your reference to Smith and Jones, all subsequent references would need renumbering to replace the deleted reference. Similarly, inserting a new reference into your report would require all subsequent reference numbers to be incremented – something that can take a long time in terms of search and replace if your word processor doesn't have a reference management system. For these reasons, if you have a choice, it is recommended that you use the Harvard system for referencing material if at all possible.

Three abbreviations that you might use when referencing are:

- *op. cit.* – in the work already cited
- *ibid.* – in the same place
- *loc. cit.* – in the place cited

Op. cit. is used to refer to an article you have cited before, earlier in your report, and is used when other references occur in between. You may have to provide the date if other authors of the same name exist. For example:

It is often said that computing is an art not a science (Johnson 1992: 22).

Smith and Jones (1993) emphasise this point when they state that 'computing has much more in common with the finer things in life, like art, than science or engineering'. However, Johnson (*op. cit:* 34) goes on to discuss ...

Ibid. is used when there are no intervening references. You must provide page numbers if required;

It is often said that computing is an art not a science (Johnson 1992). [Intervening text here but no references] ... Johnson (*ibid.*) states that computing can be defined in terms of romantic form ...

Loc. cit. is used to refer to the same page of an article you have previously cited. You should provide the date as appropriate. For example:

It is often said that computing is an art not a science (Johnson 1992: 22). Smith and Jones (1993: 20) emphasise this point when they state that 'computing has much more in common with the finer things in life, like art, than science or engineering'. However, Johnson (*loc. cit.*) goes on to discuss ...

While these abbreviations are often found in short articles and are useful when using a numeric referencing system, they should be used sparingly and with care in longer documents. Try to limit these abbreviations to references that occur on the same page or at most one page earlier in your report. Linking *ibid., op. cit.* and *loc. cit.* to a reference that occurred two or more pages beforehand makes it difficult for the reader to follow.

Above all, make sure from the way you have referenced material within your report that it is clear exactly to which article you are referring and you do not identify two articles in the same way. In addition, make sure that you use a consistent style – don't switch from Harvard form to numeric form and vice versa, and do not mix the two forms together.

6.5.2 **Listing references**

Generally speaking, the best place to list all the references you have used is at the back of your report, as opposed to footnotes at the bottom of pages or lists at the end of each chapter. This provides the reader with a single compendium of all relevant material that can be accessed easily. Articles you have used are presented under the heading of either *References* or *Bibliography*. References list only those articles that have been referred to (cited) within the report itself. A bibliography will list all the articles you have used in your project but that are not necessarily referred to in the body of the report. Bibliographies are useful for the reader in that they identify all material that is relevant for taking your work forward or understanding it in more depth. For undergraduate projects and books it might be more appropriate to include a bibliography, but for postgraduate projects it would not. Your supervisor should be able to advise you on which approach to use.

How you present references will depend on the referencing system you are using, *Harvard* or *numeric*. Only the Harvard system will be discussed in detail as the numeric system is basically the same. The only difference with the numeric system is that each reference is presented in its numerical order and is presented with its numerical identifier first. For example:

15. Wilson, G. (1992) *The Implications of Art*, Gower, London.
16. Herbert, K. (1991) *The Art of Science*, Chapman & Hall, Manchester.

In the Harvard system the use of italics, commas, colons, upper case letters, abbreviations (such as Vol for Volume) and brackets may well be dictated by your own institution's 'house' style. However, Harvard references should always be presented alphabetically with articles by the same author(s) presented chronologically. Examples are given in the following subsections.

Books

Anderson, J., Jones, J.P. and Peterson, K.K.L. (1982) *The Implications of Science*, 2nd edition, Pitman, London.
Benjamin, T. (1956) *Computer Science Made Easy*, Arnold, Leeds.

Note that it is not necessary to include terms such as 'Ltd', 'Inc.' etc. for publisher's names as long as the publisher is clearly known from the information presented. The date that is presented represents the date on which that edition of the book was *first* published. This provides an indication of the age of the book, which would not be apparent by referencing a reprint date, which could be several years later.

Journal articles

Brown, A. and Wesley, C.W. (1995a) 'An investigation of the Hawthorne effect', *Management Sciences Journal*, **42**(1), 47–66.
Brown, A. and Wesley, C.W. (1995b) 'Adaptation of genetic algorithms in Hawthorne analysis', *Management Monthly*, **28**(2), 21–23.

Notice the use of letters (1995a, 1995b) to uniquely identify these two articles produced by the same authors in the same year.

Web addresses

Gaynor, L. (1993) 'Introduction to artificial intelligence', available from Internet ⟨http://www.cai.com/ai/1086⟩ (25 July 1999).
International Group on Complex Systems (1999), 'Systems analysis', Minutes of Second Meeting, 12 June 1999, ⟨http://www.IGCS.com/Min/two.html⟩ (25 July 1999).

References to Internet sites should include the *full* web address including *http* etc. Make sure that you present the title of the page, article and site name where appropriate. These references should also include the date on which the site was accessed. Because the Internet is ever-changing, these references may become outdated very quickly.

Trade or company publications
IAEA (1983) *Guidebook on Computer Techniques in Nuclear Plants*, Technical Report Series No. 27, International Atomic Energy Agency, Russia.
National Environment Research Council (1992) *Computers in Hydrology Report*, Vol. II, NERC, London.

Theses
Hampson, J. (1994) 'The effectiveness of AI in calcite modelling', unpublished PhD thesis, Department of Computing, University of Strathclyde.

Conferences
Jowitt, J.D. (1995) 'Information systems in a progressive society', in *Applications of Information Systems XI*, Eds Cartwright, R.A. and Laurence, G., Rowntree Publications, Leeds.
ISAIS (1995) *International Symposium on Applications of Information Systems XI*, proceedings of an international conference organised by the Society of IS, London, 12–16 June 1994, Rowntree Publications, Leeds.

The first reference here (Jowitt 1995) is for an article presented at a conference. The second reference refers to the conference proceedings itself.

Television programmes
The Information Programme (1993) Channel Four Television Corporation, broadcast 8.30 p.m. Tuesday 18 November 1993.
Kay, S. (1992) *The World's a Stage*, BBC1.

The first reference here has no specific 'author' or presenter so is presented using the programme's title as a reference. The second reference is more vague, and perhaps, represents a secondary reference in which as much information as possible has been presented.

CD-ROM
Katlen, P. and Rose, P. (1992) *Information Systems in the 1990s*, CAROM CD-ROM, Solar Information Systems, London.

The references presented above are by no means comprehensive and you will undoubtedly come across an article, some data or some other material from an obscure source that is not covered by these examples. However, unless your institution has specific guidelines to follow when referencing such material, you will have to present the reference in a way that you feel is appropriate. If your supervisor is unable to help you, remember two things. First, the reference should be clear enough so that anyone reading your report knows to which article you are referring and, second, you should ensure you have provided sufficient information for the reader to trace that article easily if he or she wishes.

6.6 Documenting software

6.6.1 *Introduction*

The documentation required to support a piece of software can be immense and covers a vast range of issues, from internal commenting of program code, systems analyses and design notes, figures and system documentation, to test plans and user guides. The following list itemises topics and documentation you might be expected to cover and include in your project to support any software that you produce:

- An introduction/overview: simple introduction to the program, what it does, who it is for.
- Technical solution adopted: what technical solution has been implemented, whether it is ideal, whether an alternative exists.
- Design: systems analysis, systems design, human factors, story boards etc.
- Software engineering information: program design, structure, definition languages, test plans etc.
- Development approach used: evolutionary delivery, build and fix etc.
- Problems encountered: bugs, errors, uncompleted sections of code.
- Limitations: what limitations there are to the program; for example, it can only handle files of a certain size, it only calculates results to an accuracy of 10% etc.
- Hardware/software requirements for running the program.
- Next stage: if you were to continue, or somebody else were to take over your project from you, which parts of the software should be developed next? Which parts of the program could be enhanced with new features? Are the code, documentation and comments and so on at a level whereby somebody could take over from you easily in the future?
- Evaluation of the software: how well does it do what it is supposed to do? Does it satisfy the user's needs?
- User guide: written at the right level of detail for the intended user.

Depending on the nature of your project, you will have to present more or less detail in each of these areas. How you complete documentation such as designs, analyses and test plans is beyond the scope of this book as it is dependent upon the development process, the methods employed and the type of project you have undertaken. For example, a pure programming project would require comprehensive analysis diagrams, test plans and system documentation, whereas a project merely developing a piece of code as a vehicle for presenting some ideas would not. The focus here is on commenting programs and writing user guides as these should be included with any piece of code you produce.

6.6.2 *Commenting program code*

Commenting program code is dependent on the programming language used (for example, a third or fourth generation language, an object oriented language, a formal language and so on), the style of code being developed and the requirements of your course and project. Having said this, there are a number of general guidelines you can follow when commenting your code:

- Understand the purpose of the program you are writing. Who is going to use it, maintain or enhance it, mark it? What is their level of knowledge? If you are merely writing a small program for your own use to test out some ideas you will not need as many comments as for a program that is going to be used and enhanced by somebody else.
- Try to ensure that you provide the right level of comments within your program – don't over-comment or under-comment and avoid comments on every single line of code. Comments should tell the programmer something that is not clear from the code itself and they are not there to explain the programming language used. Provided you have used suitable variable names and a logical structure for your program then comments should be limited.
- It is advisable to comment each function, procedure, object, block, screen and so on (depending on the language used). This will explain, at the very least, what each main component of your program does and may be the depth of commenting required by someone to understand how the program works and is structured.
- Try to make comments stand out from your code so that they don't become buried as a mass of text in your program. For example, tab each *in-line* comment clear of the code to the right and keep line spaces around *full-line* comments.
- Avoid long winded explanations. Keep comments brief and clear – you are not writing an essay.
- Avoid wasting time producing fancy borders, header styles and so on. Your comments are there to provide understanding and explanation to your program; they are not there to make it look pretty.
- Make sure you include vital information at the start of your program such as author, date, version number, a description of what the program

does and, possibly, a brief explanation of how it does it. These comments are often included as *block* comments – several lines of full-line comments providing more detailed explanation.
- Try to make sure that you maintain and update program comments as you amend and develop your software. There is little point in keeping outdated comments in your code that refer to much earlier and different versions of your program.

In summary, it is probably a good idea to get guidance from your supervisor as to the style and level of comments required. Your department may have guidelines on what is expected in the form of program comments and there may be an 'in house' style you have to follow.

6.6.3 **Writing user guides**

There has been a lot of research in recent years into user guides: their structure, presentation and content, usability, trainability, minimalist training issues and so on, all of which are beyond the intended scope of this book. In this case you are more likely to be interested in user guides from a narrower perspective in that your guide is not going to be used by the 'masses' but within your own institution as part of your computing project and part of its assessment.

In this context any user guides you develop are likely to be presented within separate documents to your final report or included within its appendices. How you present user guides is up to you but the longer they are the more sensible it will be to present them as separate documents. Get advice from your supervisor on the scope of any documentation required. Whatever the case, they should provide the user with at least these pieces of information:

- an overview of the software: what it does, who it is intended for.
- an idea of its hardware requirements: memory requirements, disk space required, additional hardware requirements such as sound cards, platform requirements (PC, Macintosh etc.), operating system requirements etc.
- how to load/install the software.
- how to start the software.
- how to end and perhaps delete/remove the software.
- details of any known problems and restrictions imposed by the program.

More broadly speaking, according to Rogerson (1989: 87), a user manual should satisfy three aims:

- 'provide practical information about the software when help is not at hand';
- 'help inexperienced users get started quickly and with least difficulty';
- 'help experienced users become productive quickly'.

When writing user guides as part of your project you should begin by identifying your target audience. Will you need a comprehensive guide so that complete beginners will be able to understand your software or will a simple overview of its functionality be sufficient as it will only ever be used by your supervisor?

User manuals tend to come in two different forms: first, *training manuals*, where the user is taught how to use the software through a number of examples that build on one another, and second, *reference manuals*, whereby experienced users can 'dip into' the manual at appropriate points for clarification or explanation of specific features of the program. How you structure your documentation will be based largely on your intended users. For experienced users a reference manual may be all that is required. However, for inexperienced users, evolutionary examples may be more appropriate. In addition, depending on the nature of your user you may have to provide detailed explanations describing simpler operating principles such as 'save as', 'page setup' etc. It is also a good idea to include some screen dumps from your program in a user guide so that users feel they are following your guide correctly when it appears that things aren't happening as they would expect. It also provides users with additional confidence to see things mapping out on the screen in the same way they are presented on paper. You might also wish to include a description of possible mistakes that could be made by a user and how the user can avoid or overcome them.

6.7 Summary

- When you begin to write your report consider the reader and be aware of any limitations on its length. Use a top-down approach to structure your report and allow sections within your report to evolve over time. There is a particular order in which you should write your report and a specific way in which it should be structured. Look for ways of practising and improving your writing style.
- Your abstract should be one of the last things that you write. It should be clear and concise, summarising the context, scope and contribution of your report. Avoid presenting your abstract as a contents listing.
- Charts and graphs can do much to enhance the appearance and content of a report. They should be used appropriately (in terms of necessity and type) and each one should be uniquely labelled and titled. You must also ensure that you scale them correctly in order to clarify the point you are trying to portray.
- The Harvard system is the most appropriate system to use for referencing material within your report. Each article should be uniquely identifiable and each reference should be complete so that the reader can trace the article.

- Documenting software covers a multitude of topics, from commenting program code to writing user guides. This chapter has focused on the development of user guides, which are usually presented as training manuals (with worked examples) or reference manuals (for more experienced users).

6.8 Further reading

Collier, J.H. (ed.) (1997) *Scientific and Technical Communication*, Sage, London.
Creme, P. and Lea, M.R. (1997) *Writing at University: A Guide for Students*, Open University Press, Buckingham.
Reynolds, L. and Simmonds, D. (1984) *Presentation of Data in Science*, Kluwer, Lancaster.
Shortland, M. and Gregory, J. (1991) *Communicating Science: A Handbook*, Longman, Harlow.

6.9 Exercises

1. Produce a report breakdown structure for your own project.
2. Write a short abstract of around 200 words for an article you have read recently. Compare your abstract with the one included with the article. Do you think your abstract is better or worse and why?
3. Collect some data from your library on your own institution; for example, number of students entering the university each year, their age, qualifications etc. How are these data presented? Enter these data into a spreadsheet and present them in a different way. Do you think that your presentation is better or worse? Why?

CHAPTER 7
Presentation skills

Aims
To introduce the skills needed to present your project effectively in oral form.

Learning objectives
When you have completed this chapter, you should be able to:

- understand how to structure, plan, and present effective oral presentations;
- demonstrate your software professionally;
- understand the purpose of, and be able to plan for, viva voce examinations.

7.1 Introduction

One of the most important aspects of any project is being able to present your findings to others. There is no point in performing an excellent piece of research if the results cannot be disseminated. While dissemination usually takes place through written reports and articles, quite often you will be called upon to make oral presentations of your work. This chapter covers the skills needed to make effective oral presentations; how to prepare them, how to structure them and how best to deliver them.

As a computing student, you will probably be involved with the development of a piece of software, a program or an entire software package. Presenting and demonstrating software falls within the theme of this chapter and is discussed in detail in Section 7.3.

You may also find that, as part of your course, you will have to attend a viva voce or oral examination. How to prepare for, and conduct yourself, during this kind of examination is discussed in Section 7.4.

7.2 Oral presentations

7.2.1 Introduction

Oral presentations are often an essential part of many degree courses these days. They are frequently used to assess students' understanding of their work and their abilities to present their findings to others in oral form.

For many people, their only involvement or encounter with you and your project will be at your oral presentation. They may be interested in your work from a professional or personal viewpoint or they may be part of the assessment team who are evaluating your work. Whatever the case, you should be trying to interest and inspire people in your work and be emphasising your own interest and enthusiasm in your project.

An oral presentation can be compared with an iceberg – most of which is always hidden from view below the surface of the ocean. Like an iceberg, your audience will only ever see 10% of the work of your presentation – the delivery itself. They will not see the other 90% of effort that you put in to preparing your presentation. Similarly, of all the material that you obtain, and all the results that you acquire during the course of your project, you might only have time to present the more interesting and most important 10% of detail.

There are a number of considerations that should be made for oral presentations: preparation, the content, visual aids you might wish to use, the delivery of the presentation itself, and how to deal with questions. The following sections deal with each of these points in turn before presenting a few final tips that can help you present your project to the best of your ability in oral form.

7.2.2 Preparation

The first stage of any oral presentation is clearly preparation. The first stage of preparation is to clarify your presentation's objectives, taking into account the audience who will be attending the presentation and the time you have available (including time for questions). If you don't know these things it is important that you clarify them as soon as possible as they will have a significant bearing on what you decide to include and leave out.

- *Objectives.* Begin by clarifying the objectives of your presentation. What do you hope to achieve with it and what should your focus be? Will you be discussing your project itself rather than its outcomes? For example, its problems, solutions, how you performed the project and so on? Alternatively, you may be presenting the technical outcomes of your project to a more scientific audience. In this case you might address points such as how the work was performed, what supporting research there is, what its context is, what you discovered, and what your results were.

Cryer (1996: 131) identifies some additional possibilities that might represent the main purpose of your presentation:

- to explain what you have achieved and, if applicable, what you intend to do next;
- to obtain advice and feedback;
- a forum for learning and mutual support;
- as part of your assessment or as a monitoring process.

- *Time*. You will probably find that your presentation will be required to last anywhere between ten minutes and one hour. Quite clearly, with only ten minutes for a presentation, you will have to get straight to the point you intend to make, while with an hour to play with, you will be able to cover more background and build up to the main point of your talk.

  You will need to clarify how much time there will be available for your presentation and how much time there will be for questions. Will you be able to decide on the proportion of time allocated for the presentation and the questions or is this specified? How flexible is this time? Is it fixed to within one or two minutes or can you over- or under-run to a much greater extent?

- *Audience*. The number and type of people who will be attending your presentation will have a significant bearing on its style and content. You should ask yourself these questions: Are they assessing you? Are they your peers? Are you hoping to inspire them with your work and persuade them to become involved with it? What do they already know? What do you want to teach them? What do you want to show them?

Now that you have an idea of the objectives, time and audience of your presentation you can move on to preparing the presentation itself. If you are struggling with ideas on what to include, begin by brainstorming ideas and writing them down on a piece of paper. Annotate each of these ideas onto a single piece of paper or peel-off sticker. You can then go about arranging your material into a logical structure – don't just expect to write a few notes down at random and expect to *ad lib* your way through them on the day. Remember that your presentation should have a beginning, a middle and an end, and points that you may be trying to get across may need some build-up or explanation first. For example, if you wanted to discuss the application of artificial intelligence techniques to air traffic control scheduling, you would do well to provide some background on these two subjects separately first, before focusing on the main point of your talk – the overlap of these two topics.

The next stage of your preparation will be to develop the visual aids you want to use. Rogerson (1989: 94) states that people retain only 10% of what they hear but 50% of what they see. Thus, visual aids are important for getting your message across and helping your audience to remember what you have presented afterwards. Visual aids can include overhead transparencies, slides, whiteboards and blackboards, computer-based presentation packages, and physical objects that you wish to show or pass around the audience. Preparation of these visual aids is discussed in more detail in Section 7.2.4.

With your talk physically prepared, the last stage of preparation is to compose yourself mentally by rehearsing your talk again and again. You may well find that you have developed too much material or are trying to cover too much detail, so you should prune your presentation to the time available. You must also familiarise yourself with the room and equipment you will be using. You should make sure that you can answer the following questions:

- Do you know how to use the overhead projector (can you access the spare bulb)?
- Can you operate the hardware for projecting computer images?
- Do you know how the slide projector works – going forward and back through the slides?
- Do you know which way up to insert slides or which way round transparencies should be placed on the projector?

You can begin initial rehearsals in the privacy of your own room or in front of a mirror to check things like timing, structure and flow. Try to rehearse your presentation in front of somebody else as well at some stage. Other people can usually spot silly mistakes or places where they feel you aren't explaining yourself clearly. Finally, try to rehearse your presentation in the room you will actually be using for the presentation. Make sure that you can use all the equipment that is there.

One cautionary note to end with is that oral presentations can often suffer from *over*-preparation. Sometimes presentations appear stilted; the off-the-cuff remarks appear well-rehearsed, the talk doesn't flow naturally, the speaker appears to be reading from a well-rehearsed script rather than talking to the audience. Try not to fall into this trap by learning your presentation word for word. The audience expect to be spoken to as people, not read to from a script. Remember that they are all individuals and expect to be spoken to as such rather than as an amorphous group.

7.2.3 *The presentation content*

All presentations should have three main sections – the beginning, the middle and the end. The purpose of the beginning is to set the scene and tone for the audience and provide them with information about your presentation's content. To cover all the points necessary for your introduction try applying the *who, what, how, why, when* approach:

- *Who* are you? What is your affiliation? Why are you there?
- *What* are you going to talk about?

- *How* long will the presentation last?
- *Why* should they listen to you? Why is what you are going to say important and timely?
- *When* can they ask questions – during the talk or at the end?

It is useful to have an introductory slide for these points. You might then like to set the scene in more detail by identifying the specific topics you will be discussing. A slide with the structure of your talk and its content is also useful here.

Having set the scene for your presentation you can move on to the main body of your talk. What you include within your presentation will clearly depend on the points discussed earlier – its objectives, the audience and the time that is available. A common approach for most talks of any reasonable length (twenty minutes or more) is to cover three main points during their main body. People can easily retain three main ideas; more will become confused and mixed in their minds.

You should always conclude and summarise your presentation – never end abruptly. Try to summarise what you have covered. What were the main points you made that you would like people to remember? What are the conclusions from your work? How do you feel the work can be developed in the future? Try to end your presentation on a high. Many people switch off during the main body of a presentation, listening mainly to the introduction and the conclusions. Don't end your talk stating that you wish you'd never pursued your project in the first place. Try to emphasise the main contributions you have made.

Try to make sure that your audience remembers your talk by giving them something to take away with them. This could be a copy of some of your slides but, perhaps, more importantly, it should be something distinctive about your talk they will remember – an unusual diagram, an explosive demonstration, or some earth shattering results.

7.2.4 *Visual aids*

As noted earlier, visual aids come in various kinds – overhead transparencies, slides, whiteboards and blackboards, and computer-based presentation packages. The most common of these is the overhead transparency, which is now used widely throughout academia and industry. More and more common these days, however, are computer-based presentations based on tools such as Microsoft PowerPoint. However, although these packages can produce very neat, colourful and dynamic images, without adequate projection equipment they are useless. The rules for presenting computer-based presentations are much the same as for producing overhead transparencies. The layout and presentation of these are discussed here.

Although blackboards and whiteboards are used extensively within teaching environments, they are not always well suited to presentations. You will find yourself continually turning your back to the audience to draw or write something, you may find yourself talking to the board rather than the audience, and if your handwriting isn't particularly neat, your jottings may be illegible anyway. However, they can be useful if you have previously drawn or written something on them before you start your presentation or need to develop an idea or a list with audience participation. Having said this, unless you are confident with these media, it is best to avoid the use of blackboards and whiteboards during presentations.

For overhead transparencies there are a number of simple considerations that you should bear in mind during their preparation:

- *Detail.* Try to make sure that your transparencies are not too detailed or too sparse. Rogerson (1989: 95) suggests that 40–50 words per transparency can be absorbed in one go.
- *Font.* Use a clear font of an adequate size. Don't use a gothic font or a size that is so small it cannot be read easily from the back of the room. The way to decide on a suitable font is to try out a sample transparency in the room beforehand. In a smaller room you might well get away with a 14 point font, but in larger auditoriums you will not.
- *Colours.* Be careful when using colours on your transparencies. Some colours clash quite badly and others do not show up very well when projected. Once again, experiment to find out which combinations are most suitable. As a general rule, bold, deep colours stand out best of all and contrasting colours between foreground text and background should be used.
- *Handwriting.* Try to avoid using handwritten or hand drawn diagrams on transparencies if at all possible. Word processed and computer generated transparencies look far more professional and appear much clearer.
- *Orientation.* It is often argued that transparencies should be presented in landscape rather than portrait format. This will clearly depend on the content of the transparency. Try to be consistent and stick with a portrait layout if possible.
- *Bullet points.* Some of the most clear transparencies are those with a few bullet points on them which you talk around during your presentation. These points provide focus for the talk and are not so detailed that the audience spends more time trying to read the transparency than listening to you.
- *Style.* Try to produce a consistent style for your transparencies – a consistent background and text colour, a consistent font, a border style perhaps including your name, affiliation and presentation title. A consistent style looks more professional and the audience don't have to keep 'acclimatising' themselves to ever-changing formats.
- *Curling.* Although not a problem with computer presentations, curling

transparencies can often cause problems when placed on the hot surface of overhead projectors. Some transparencies come with cardboard sides so this is not a problem. However, others, particularly those on which you have left a paper strip attached, curl almost in half. The solution is simply to carry a few coins to place on the edges of the transparency to weight it down, or, alternatively, use a pen.

Two other aids you might wish to consider are handouts and objects that can be passed around the audience. Before you pass out handouts you should be aware of their purpose. If the audience will need the handouts during your presentation to refer to you should pass them out before you begin. If not, it is best to leave them until the end as they can cause a lot of distraction to you and the audience during your presentation.

Passing around objects (for example, circuit boards) is quite interesting for the audience as it gives them a hands-on, close up view of what you are talking about. They can, however, cause an unwelcome distraction so be careful as to the number of objects you pass around (especially if they are fragile!) and when you do it. Try to hand objects around during less intense periods of your talk, when the audience's complete attention is not required.

7.2.5 Delivery

Although you might be well prepared and your visual aids look stunning, a poor delivery can ruin your presentation. Rogerson (1989: 97) identifies a number of factors that can distract the audience from what you are saying during delivery:

- Talking with your back to the audience or mumbling. Lots of 'mmms' and 'errs';
- Not scanning the audience as a whole but focusing on one part of the room only;
- Wild gesticulation – people focus on this rather than what you are saying;
- Irrelevant information or sidetracking from the main point;
- Extraneous noise.

In addition, you might also be trying to cover too much detail in a particular area – perhaps presenting lots of statistics, detailed equations and so on. Figure 7.1 provides an indication of audience attention during a presentation's delivery. As you can see, many people only remain focused at the beginning, when they are wide awake, and towards the end, when they wake up and try to catch up on what you are saying. Your delivery has a distinct effect on the audience's attention during the main body of your presentation.

- *Scanning*. Make sure that you scan around all the audience during your presentation and remember to talk to people, not just their faces. Quite

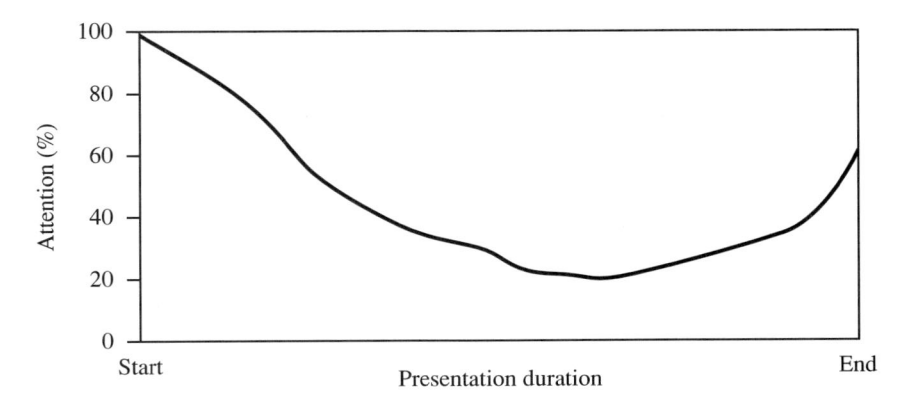

Figure 7.1 *An audience's attention level during a presentation*

often you will see two or three people paying close attention to what you are saying, perhaps nodding in agreement or taking notes. You will tend to find that you focus on these people. It then feels as if you are almost talking to one person at a time, not a large group and this can help reduce your nerves.
- *All clear.* When you put transparencies onto the overhead projector or project slides from your computer, make sure that they are clear. Make sure that you are not in the way, the slides are the right way up and everything is in focus.
- *Handovers.* If you are involved with a joint presentation, for example as part of a group project, make sure that the handovers to each other are rehearsed and you know the sequence in which each of you is speaking. It looks very unprofessional to see people end their section abruptly and ask the rest of the group 'who's next?'.
- *Voice.* Make sure that you maintain a clear, confident voice throughout your presentation and don't mumble. Take deep breaths, slow down and pause to compose yourself if you have to.
- *Timing.* Make sure that you keep to time during your presentation. Keep a watch or a clock within sight and know the time when you are due to finish.
- *Pauses.* Pauses can be used to good effect during a presentation. The audience will pay close attention to what you have to say after a pause so use them just before you have something important to say. Try not to use too many or they will lose their effect.

One other factor you will want to consider as part of your delivery is how to use your notes. Many people use a series of cards with points set down on each of them covering the content of their talk. Quite often, however, people get ahead of themselves, and are often seen rummaging through their cards to see what they are supposed to be talking about next. Alternatively, you can have your notes written down on the backing sheet of each transparency you use. These might direct you towards the points that you want to make for that transparency. Another approach is to have one or two sheets of paper nearby with the main points and structure of your talk noted down to prompt you, possibly with lines and arrows to direct you.

It is up to you how much detail you put down on your cards or sheets. With practice, just a few prompting words should be sufficient. At the other extreme you might want to write down your talk word for word in case you dry up and have to read it out but this is ill advised. Although you should make the notes detailed enough so that you know what to say, they shouldn't be so detailed that you have to stop your presentation to read them. A cursory glance should be all that is required for a well-rehearsed presentation.

7.2.6 Dealing with questions

Although you might complete your presentation satisfactorily, quite often the hardest part of an oral presentation is fielding the questions at the end. This is the part over which you have little control. In some circumstances, particularly if your presentation forms part of your assessment, the questioners know the answers to the questions they pose. They are probing your depth of knowledge and ability to convey that knowledge. They are also interested to see how you handle questions and how well you can 'think on your feet'.

A few points worth considering that will help you to deal with questions are:

- *Preparation.* Try to think beforehand what kinds of questions you might be asked. Will they be technical or more general? What kinds of answers will you be expected to give – extended answers or short answers? Will you be expected to justify or defend parts of your project?
- *Plants.* It is not uncommon for presenters to 'plant' questions with colleagues in the audience. This can help to relax you because you have the prepared answers, and can take up time that might otherwise have been filled with more difficult questions.
- *Confidence.* At all times try to remain confident. You have been asked to speak for a reason so you are justified in being there and people feel you are worthy to be asked a question.
- *Brevity.* Try to keep your answers brief and to the point.
- *Conflict.* Avoid conflict with the audience. Admit that differences do exist, discuss alternative interpretations and opinions, and try to address things from a higher level. In addition, avoid apportioning blame. If some results came out unexpectedly or some aspects of your project didn't conclude satisfactorily explain why this happened from your perspective. Don't blame person x or person y – your project is your responsibility so justify it from this angle.

- *Clarification.* You should always ask for clarification if you haven't understood a question. Don't try to answer what you think was asked or the question you would like to answer. Questioners will usually probe you further until they receive the response they are looking for.
- *Offer to speak to the questioner later.* If you are really struggling with a question or really don't understand it you can offer to speak to the questioner in more detail later.
- *Address the audience.* When you answer questions make sure that you address your answer to the whole audience. Your presentation isn't over and you still have a responsibility to speak to the entire audience rather than entering an intimate conversation with one individual.

The chair of your presentation's session will often step in if questioning becomes hostile. This is very rare but it does happen on occasions. If you feel you are being victimised or insulted you should ask the chair to intervene on your behalf.

7.2.7 Presentation tips

To conclude, a few tips are presented that are worth considering to improve your oral presentations.

- *Time.* If you have difficulty keeping to time (either over- or underestimating) have some spare transparencies you can 'drop in' or take out of your presentation depending on how time is progressing.
- *Pointers.* Try to avoid using laser pointers. They are never clear and wobble all over the screen you are trying to point at. A much better way is to use a pen or pointer on the overhead projector itself. If you are nervous, place the pen down against the point you are referring to and leave it there.
- *Movement.* Many people fidget and move around alarmingly when they are giving a presentation. With practice you can suppress these urges and learn to avoid annoying habits such as jangling keys in your pocket. If you are going to make a movement try not to make it an exaggerated one unless you need to do so for emphasis and to demonstrate your enthusiasm. If you want to stop yourself walking around, place a finger on the nearest desk or chair – subconsciously your body will want to remain fixed where you are.
- *Nerves.* Everybody suffers from nerves to some extent or another. While nerves are never totally eliminated, they do ebb as you become more and more used to giving presentations. The tip here is to give as many presentations as possible and practise as much as possible. The more you do, the easier it becomes. Without a few nerves you will not have enough adrenalin to give an exciting presentation. If you are

shaking you could perhaps switch the overhead projector off as you change slides.
- *Bulbs blowing*. Overhead projectors are not infallible and the bulbs do blow in them quite frequently. Quite often they have spare bulbs within them that you can switch to, so learn how to do this. Alternatively, have a contingency plan such as using a whiteboard or referring to handouts of your slides. Usually, however, if the overhead projector does break down, your session chair will step in to assist you.

In conclusion, above all else, be *enthusiastic*. Enthusiasm can do a lot to hide nerves and perhaps some content lacking from your presentation. The audience will remain on the edge of their seats when they see how interested you are in your work and will become motivated and supportive of you as well.

7.3 Demonstrating software

7.3.1 Introduction

As a student on a computing course of one kind or another, there is a strong chance that you will have to develop a piece of software at some stage. Whether this software is the main component of your project or whether it is merely a vehicle for testing out and presenting some ideas, you may well have to demonstrate this software to your tutor, your peers, a client or some other interested parties. This section discusses ways to prepare for such a presentation, some considerations you should make before your demonstration and some tips that will assist you.

7.3.2 Preparation

You should prepare for a software demonstration in much the same way as you would prepare an oral presentation. You should decide on your demonstration's purpose, then plan, prepare and rehearse your demonstration.

When deciding on your demonstration's purpose ask yourself what you hope to achieve. What do you hope to show and get across to the audience?

Your demonstration should also be planned thoroughly. Structure the demonstration beforehand – don't just expect to 'play around' with your program on the day. Like an oral presentation, it should have a beginning, a middle and an end. You should also decide how you want the demonstration to be performed:

- *Solo running*. This involves you running through a particular, planned sequence of tasks on your own without allowing interruptions or audience interaction. This approach is not advisable as it might appear that you are 'protecting' your program's weaknesses by merely

demonstrating some simplistic features. In other words, any variations to the sequence or the data you are entering might cause your program to crash. Although this might not be the case, this might come across to the audience. If your tutor tested, marked or used your software at a later date and found all these errors, it would appear as if you were trying to hide them.
- *Rolling demonstration.* The software runs itself through a predetermined demonstration that cannot be interacted with. This might be a demonstration package you have developed rather than the software package itself.
- *Audience participation.* Allowing the audience to request things or suggest examples as you run through the program in a relatively free manner. This is the most common approach to software demonstrations where you have an approximate idea of the functions and options you wish to demonstrate but expect to be directed some times by audience requests.
- *Audience running.* Allowing the audience to play with the software with you guiding them. This approach is suitable for a software tool that is demonstrating usability and ease of learning.

When you prepare your demonstration you should bear three things in mind – *time*, *audience* and *focus*:

- *Time.* How much time is available? You do not want to over- or under-run your demonstration so careful preparation and timing of actions during rehearsal is important. If you are over-running think about parts of the program that don't really need demonstrating. Can you go straight to the part of the program you really want the audience to see and skip any introductory screens or messages?
- *Audience.* Know who the audience will be. What do they know? What do they want to see or learn? Are they staff, students or a client? What will you have to explain? What is the audience likely to ask you? Will you need to justify primary things such as the choice of programming language used, the algorithm you have decided to use and so on?

It may be that you are presenting your software to your tutor but the software is actually for somebody else – an industrial client, for example. Your tutor, therefore, may be more interested in your design, interface development and so on, whereas the client may be more interested in learning how the software works.

The size of group will also have a bearing on your presentation. According to Rogerson (1989: 103), a software demonstration to a large group 'will be more generalised and more high level than that to a smaller group when the interests can be identified and the demonstration tailored accordingly'. The size of audience will also have an effect on the choice of hardware you will need to use. For three or

four people a single monitor might be suitable, but for larger groups you will have to consider using a projection system of some kind or another.
- *Focus*. Concentrate and focus on the good points of your software, not just basic functions such as loading and saving files, printing and so on. Similarly, try to focus the demonstration towards the purpose of your project. For example, if your project aimed to explore human–computer interaction issues, concentrate on the software's screen designs, layouts and navigation routes. If it was to implement and test a particular algorithm, focus on the results and outputs from the software and its efficiency.

Before you actually perform your demonstration you should rehearse it thoroughly, preferably on the hardware system you will be using on the day. Make sure that your software will work on the system you will be using. Is it the right hardware configuration? Does it need a graphics card? And so on.

7.3.3 **The demonstration**

Provided that you have prepared well, hopefully all will go well on the day. However, it is often the case that things go wrong or not according to plan in oral presentations. This is especially the case in software demonstrations.

If possible, try to set up as much as you can beforehand. People hate to wait around while you load software, set up overhead projectors and so on. If this is not possible try to practice loading your software somewhere else so that you can load it as quickly and easily as possible. Although your presentation may not yet have started, people can be put off your program before they have even seen it working because it appears to need half an hour and a PhD to install! Alternatively, be prepared to give a small anecdote, story or some additional information about your program to help pass the time while it loads.

Make sure that all the audience can see the screen clearly. Is there any reflective light on the screen? Is the monitor clear of smudges and finger marks?

7.3.4 **Demonstration tips**

The following points are a selection of tips that will help you prepare and present effective software demonstrations. This list is not exhaustive and the effectiveness of individual tips will depend on the type of demonstration you are performing, the programming language you have used, and the audience.

- Know your software's limitations, bugs, and faults so that you don't try to do something that your software can't handle. This is also useful if you are to demonstrate a particular aspect of the code in which there are problems so you don't look embarrassed or surprised when things go wrong. In this case you can explain that that section is still under

development or hasn't been thoroughly tested yet. You can also state that the fault/bug is known and is documented on page 11 of the report!
- Know how your software works and how it is structured. This will enable you to explain these points if asked and will demonstrate your deeper understanding of the code.
- If your software is well written and well structured it may well consist of a number of *stubs*. These stubs are sections of code (components and functions) that haven't been completed but will be developed in the future. Developing a program using a top-down approach to identify its components and functions is a recognised practice and is acceptable providing that the system doesn't crash when it accesses these stubs. In these cases it is usual for each stub to return a message such as 'This function is still under development'. Developing your program in this way improves its maintainability, readability and structure.
- Highlight some additional features you have included that may not be apparent from a straightforward demonstration. For example, if the software asks the user to enter a month number, the software ensures the value is between 1 and 12. These kinds of checks, although included, are not normally evident from a demonstration unless pointed out or questioned.
- Never say 'Oh, that shouldn't have happened' or 'What's happening now?'.
- Be aware of similar packages. Know the competition and understand how your software compares with and improves on them. Section 4.3 provided some guidance on where to look for software relevant to your project.
- Practise beforehand. The main point to emphasise is rehearsal. You don't want to run out of time having only demonstrated half of your program and you don't want to come across unexpected bugs.

7.4 Viva voce examinations

Not only do students often have to present their projects in oral presentations but they also have to 'defend' their project during a viva voce examination. This form of examination is more common at postgraduate level and is compulsory for PhDs.

A *viva* is an oral 'interview' conducted by examiners. Sometimes it is used merely to check that the work of the project is your own and has not been done by someone else. Sometimes it is used to clarify some points you made in your report that are vague or unclear. It is more commonly used to assess your understanding, depth of knowledge, confidence and ability to present your project in an examination situation. You should be prepared to defend your project during the examination, justifying why it is important and timely. You should also be able to explain and discuss the contribution that your project is making. You will not be expected to know your report/dissertation word for word (for example, what is on page 10, paragraph 2) and you should be able to refer to your report during the examination.

In some cases the viva is used only to upgrade your mark; for example, if you are a borderline case and the examiner is looking for a good reason to increase your final mark. At postgraduate level the viva is used as an additional way of examining your understanding of your project and the subject area, and provides further evidence to support your project.

The nature of your course will affect the duration and content of any viva you might have to attend. Vivas can last for anything from five to ten minutes to several hours or even two or three days in the case of some PhDs. For open-ended vivas, generally speaking, the shorter they are, the more confident the examiners are with the quality of your work and the less they feel they need to probe you on your understanding.

Who conducts the examination will also be dictated by your course's requirements. At one extreme it might be little more than a brief chat with your supervisor. For postgraduate research degrees it is more than likely that external examiners will conduct the viva, with internal examiners and possibly your own supervisor in attendance. For undergraduate projects, external examiners are unlikely and your own supervisor or another academic within your department will conduct the interview.

Whether your viva is a short interview with your supervisor or the more formal postgraduate viva, you should still prepare for it thoroughly:

- Make sure that you read your report thoroughly beforehand so that it is fresh in your mind. For postgraduate projects there can often be a gap of several months between the time you complete and submit your dissertation and the time you attend your viva.
- Try to identify any errors, omissions and perhaps shortfalls with your work, so that you are prepared to defend these points in the examination. If an examiner identifies a shortfall with your work of which you were unaware it can catch you off guard and leave you struggling. If, however, you have identified any problems beforehand, you can perhaps be prepared to discuss why you didn't do something in a particular way or feel that such and such a method was inappropriate in your case. You could then move on to emphasise some of the more important findings you made.
- Be aware of the things you left out of your report – references, data, methods and so on. Be prepared to defend your reasons for omitting them.
- Be prepared to discuss future developments to your work. Where do you feel your research is heading? What do you think is the future of your

subject area? What topics do you feel are suitable for further research and development? If you are unable to do this you might give the impression that your project has been merely a vehicle for obtaining your degree and you have no motivation towards the work or enough interest to care how it is developed in the future.
- Be prepared to answer quite general questions about your project: 'Tell me about your project', 'Which part of your project did you enjoy the most?' and so on (Cryer 1996: 193). These kinds of questions can often cause more problems than the highly technical questions on specific aspects of your project that you understand in detail and can talk about for hours.
- Make sure that you understand the broader subject area in which your project resides. This will allow you to emphasise the contribution that your project is making and enable you to discuss its context within wider issues.

During the examination;

- Make sure that you defend your project positively. In other words, don't criticise the work of others but focus on the contribution that your own project is making. You should show that you do take the work of others seriously even if you disagree with them (Cryer 1996: 197).
- Be prepared to answer open questions and give extended answers, not just simple 'yes' or 'no' answers. Ricketts (1998: 25) presents some typical questions you might encounter in your viva that require extended answers. Typical questions include:
  - What related research did you locate and draw on?
  - What do you feel was the most challenging part of your project?
  - What was the most interesting part of your project?
  - What is the main contribution your project is making?
  - What would you do differently next time?
  - What makes you think your project is the right level (in terms of scope, breadth, depth, quality) for your course?
- Avoid confrontation. Don't argue with the examiners but try to explain your point of view and why you feel things are the way you see them. The examiners will expect you to argue your case, but not aggressively.

Cryer (1996: 197) presents some additional guidelines for conducting yourself during your viva:

- Take a notepad and pen to the viva if you feel this will help.
- Take your own copy of the report/dissertation with you to refer to during the examination. You might also wish to include some annotated

notes to provide yourself with prompts – for example, why you did things in particular ways, why you chose this method, how you implemented this algorithm and so on. However, try to avoid reading directly from your report during the viva (Ricketts 1998: 26).
- Remain composed. Be pleasant and polite and sit squarely on the chair.
- Listen attentively to the examiners and ask for clarification if you need it.

Cryer (1996: 196) also presents some suggestions on how you should dress for an oral examination. She suggests that you should 'choose clothes that are smart and businesslike, to show that you appreciate the importance of the occasion'. However, you shouldn't try to upstage your examiners and in certain circumstances casual dress would be quite acceptable, but confirm this with your supervisor beforehand.

Overall, remember not to panic during your viva. The examiners are not trying to catch you out, but merely trying to probe your understanding about your work and clarify some of the ideas and points that you have made. Bear this in mind and think of your viva as an *opportunity* to put forward your own views on the subject and support the work you have accomplished.

7.5 Summary

- Oral presentations are quite common within most computing degree courses. You must prepare for such presentations thoroughly. Begin by deciding on the objectives of your presentation and make sure you know who the audience will be and how much time you have available. Make sure that your presentation has a logical structure with a beginning, a middle and an end. Make sure all your visual aids are clear and that you rehearse your presentation well. Some tips were presented on preparing overhead transparencies, delivering your presentation and fielding questions.
- Prepare software demonstrations in the same way that you would prepare an oral presentation. Decide on the demonstration's purpose then plan, prepare and rehearse it thoroughly. Be aware of your audience, the time you have available and what you want to focus on.
- It is not uncommon for computing students to sit viva voce examinations. Make sure that you are well prepared for such an examination – read through your report beforehand, try to think of and prepare for any questions that may be asked, know about the strengths and weaknesses of your report and understand how it fits into its wider context. During the examination you should avoid confrontation and be prepared to defend your work. You should also be able to discuss how you feel your work could be developed in the future.

7.6 **Further reading**

Campbell, J.P. (1990) *Speak for Yourself: A Practical Guide to Giving Successful Presentations, Speeches and Talks*, BBC Books, London.

Morrisey, G.L. and Sechrest, T.L. (1987) *Effective Business and Technical Presentations,* 3rd Edition, Addison-Wesley, Wokingham.

Tierney, E.P. (1996) *How to Make Effective Presentations*, Sage, London.

CHAPTER 8
Final considerations

Aims
To discuss life after your project.

Learning objectives
When you have completed this chapter, you should be able to:

- understand ways in which you can develop your project further in the future;
- understand exemption and accreditation criteria for projects by the British Computer Society;
- recognise the skills you have acquired from doing your project and understand how you can apply these skills in the future.

8.1 Introduction

Now that your project is coming to an end there are a number of things you will wish to consider for the future. Just what does the future hold for you? Are you going to stay on in academia or move on to pastures new and go into industry? Do you wish to forget all about your project or take it further? Will the successful completion of your project lead to further qualifications and recognition such as British Computer Society membership? What have you learnt from doing your project and how will these skills be useful in the future?

8.2 Taking your project further

8.2.1 Introduction

When you complete your project, hand it in and crack open the champagne. You will probably have one of two feelings about it. You might be so fed up with the sight of it that you never want to see it again and you want to burn all your books and notes. This, however, is not advisable as you may need to attend a viva or rework some of your project if things didn't go quite according to plan. Alternatively, you might be so enthusiastic about what you have achieved that you eagerly anticipate your 'A' grade and can't wait to get back to your work and develop your great ideas further.

Developing your project further can result in a number of things. You may wish to develop a commercial software package from a program that you wrote as part of your project. If you have completed an undergraduate project, you might want to develop your ideas further into an MPhil or PhD. You might want to write a paper on your work to share your ideas with the academic community. You might want to patent your work or you might want to seek some kind of funding so that you can develop your work further. Some of these issues are discussed in the following few sections.

8.2.2 Seeking funding

Trying to obtain funding for projects is not an easy task, even for experienced academics and managers. As a newly qualified graduate with little track record and probably few, if any, publications, you stand little chance of obtaining funding on your own. You also have the problem of not knowing who to turn to for funds and how to apply and complete any forms and paperwork that are required in an appropriate way. In short, you will probably not obtain funding on your own. One way around this is to try to forge links with research groups and industry. Your own department might have a research group with internationally recognised researchers who might be interested in your work and wish to involve you with theirs. Your supervisor may wish to keep you on as a research student or a research assistant. You may be lucky and have developed some software for a local company as part of your project so it might be worth liaising with them for further funds. Whatever the case, you will need to work with somebody else and learn from experience.

Applying for research funding and obtaining grants is not discussed widely and there are few texts devoted to this topic. However, two books that you may find useful to help you are Burcham and Rutherford (1987) and Ries and Leukefeld (1995), which provide a useful overview of this topic.

8.2.3 Developing commercial software packages

Because of the nature of your course it is likely that you might develop a piece of software as part of your project. You might feel that this software has some commercial value and you might wish to market it as such. This may require a lot more development work or it may simply mean packaging the software in an appropriate way for delivery. Once again, this kind of project advancement is not easy to do on your own.

You may have to establish some commercial links to market your product.

You might have to obtain some kind of funding or financial backing to get your ideas off the ground. You might also find there are difficulties with patents and intellectual property rights over work you have done for your project. These problems might be even more pronounced if your project involved working with an organisation or company and they wish to stake some claim over your work.

Whatever the case, perhaps the best place to start to resolve these issues is with your project supervisor. He or she should be able to help you or know who you should contact to address these issues. They might also be keen to be involved with any future developments that you make because they will already have been closely involved with your project to a large extent.

8.2.4 Copyright and patents

Who owns the rights to your project when you have finally submitted it for assessment is a 'grey area' within universities. Some institutions openly recognise your *intellectual property rights* (IPR). They recognise that you have intellectual property rights over any work that you produce as part of your course. The copyright for everything you produce thus belongs to you. This means that, while your institution would require copies of your work to retain for assessment purposes, you would be able to sell patent and copyrights for your work as you wished. You would also be entitled, for example, to develop and sell any software that you had produced as part of your course.

While this level of recognition of student ownership represents one extreme, other institutions will claim to own all rights to any work that is produced by students during, and as part of, an academic course. In certain instances, where collaborative projects have been undertaken with industry, you might find that the company involved with the project will wish to retain some ownership of anything that you produce as well.

In summary, if you feel that you wish to take your work further or develop something commercial from it, it is worth checking to see what rights you have over what you have produced. Check your own institution's guidelines and rules on matters of this nature and be prepared for vague answers! Patent and copyright laws are extremely complex and you may well find that you end up going round in circles and generating more questions than answers. For more information on IPR refer to Bainbridge (1995), which is an entire book devoted to the subject of intellectual property.

8.2.5 Publishing your work

You may feel that your project went so well that you wish to publish your work, either in a recognised journal or through a forthcoming conference. Your supervisor may well be closely involved with this idea and will certainly advise you. Writing for publication is not as simple as cutting and pasting a few sections from your report. It must have some form of logical structure to it and it must show clear evidence of a contribution. The process of getting work published can also be rather long winded – for example, it is common for some articles to be published well over a year after they have been submitted.

There are books available that can advise you on writing for publication. Three such texts devoted to this topic are Lester (1993), Day (1996) and Jamieson (1996), which you should consider referring to if you are thinking of writing an academic article for the first time. Alternative routes into publication can be through submitting internal reports within your own department or by writing brief summary papers or articles in more popular journals and newspapers.

8.3 Additional topics

While this book has covered probably all the topics you will require to complete both undergraduate and postgraduate computing projects successfully, there are a number of topics that have only been mentioned in passing and may be relevant or needed by you. This section briefly summarises these topics and provides you with some pointers towards further reading that you may find useful.

- *Statistics*. Part of your project may well require some form of statistical analyses. For example, from running some software speed trials, is an algorithm you have developed *significantly* better than an existing algorithm? Are any of the responses from a survey you have used 'significant'?

    The number of statistical tests available is enormous and beyond the scope of this book to discuss. There are also many books available that cover statistics. Some that you may find useful are Kanji (1993), which summarises a number of statistical tests and defines their application, and Gibson (1994), which provides a reasonable introduction to elementary statistics.

- *Questionnaire design and analysis*. As part of your project you may need to design and put together a questionnaire, decide how to use it and who to send it to, and work out how to analyse the responses. Questionnaire design and application is not a straightforward issue. However, texts that might help you with these topics include Hague (1993) and Oppenheim (1992), which both provide good coverage of this subject.

    Questionnaires may form part of a wider survey that you wish to undertake. While you will often find some information on performing surveys within more general texts, two books devoted exclusively to this topic are Fowler (1995) and Czaja and Blair (1996).

- *Qualitative analysis.* Qualitative data are those data which you gather that are not expressed in absolute arithmetical terms. They represent opinions, observations and ideas, and are generally gathered from questionnaires, surveys and interviews. Reviewing, analysing, evaluating and summarising these data often occurs in sociological studies. This may, for example, form part of an information systems project that aims to obtain user feedback on human interface issues. Two texts that cover this subject in detail are Mason (1996) and Silverman (1997).

8.4 British Computer Society exemption and accreditation

8.4.1 The British Computer Society

The British Computer Society (BCS) is the professional representative body for computer scientists and information systems practitioners within the UK. As a graduate from a computer course of one kind or another you are encouraged to join the Society because it represents your interests at a professional level. Under its Royal Charter the BCS is required to 'establish and maintain standards of professional competence, conduct and ethical practice for Information Systems Practitioners' (BCS 1998: 4).

In order to become a member of this professional body, the Society initially established the BCS examination so that potential members could demonstrate their competencies within the field. However, because of the vast range of computer qualifications available at undergraduate and postgraduate level, the Society introduced 'a system of exemptions for appropriate courses ... to provide alternative routes to Membership'.

In 1990 the Society became a nominated body of the Engineering Council so the exemption system was extended to include 'accreditation at Chartered Engineer (CEng) or Incorporated Engineer (IEng) level'. The BCS thus visits academic institutions to assess which exemptions or accreditations should be awarded for computer science and information systems courses. You will need to check with your own institution to see what level (if any) of exemptions or accreditations apply to your own particular course. You may find, for example, that while one course within your department is fully exempt, another is not.

You can become a member of the BCS at one of a number of levels. For example, to become an Associate Member you would normally have to complete Part I of the BCS examination or its equivalent. You may be exempt from completing this part of the examination because you have successfully completed a recognised HND or Honours degree. To become a Corporate Member you would have to complete Part II of the BCS examination, or have completed a recognised Honours degree successfully.

Not only must you complete the relevant BCS examination (or show you have achieved its equivalent) to become a professional member of the Society, but you must also complete a *Professional Project*. The Professional Project, like the BCS examination, must also be completed at one of two levels, depending on the type of membership to which you are applying. Thus, the Professional Project must be completed at either Level I or Level II.

Usually, as part of your course, you will be expected to complete a project of one kind or another. The Society recognises this point and exempts people who have completed an acceptable project as part of their university course from the Professional Project. Your institution might have blanket exemption by which all students who complete their course are exempt from the appropriate level of the Professional Project. Alternatively, your institution may have selective exemption in that only students who complete 'appropriate' projects will be exempt from the Professional Project. You will need to confirm the level of exemption your department holds.

Exemption and accreditation of courses depends upon a vast range of factors – their underlying theory, level of group work, project management, how they integrate theory and practice, how they work with other disciplines and so on. However, within the scope of this book computing projects are the primary concern and, as such, the Society's requirements for exemption from the Professional Project are presented.

8.4.2 **Exemption from the Professional Project**

The Society requires that in order for projects to meet the requirements for exemption they 'must be passed at the first attempt to gain the award, with no condonement and no referral'. The Society also identifies what your project's report should contain. The following list is taken directly from the BCS guidelines (1998: 10):

- 'elucidation of the problem and the objectives of the project';
- 'an in-depth investigation of the context/literature/other similar products';
- 'a clear description of the stages of the life cycle undertaken';
- 'a description of the use of appropriate tools to support the development process';
- 'a description of how verification and validation were applied at all stages';
- 'a critical appraisal of the project, indicating the rationale for design/implementation decisions, lessons learnt ... and evaluation (with hindsight) of the product and the process of its production';
- 'in the case of group projects, a clear indication of the part played by the author in achieving the goals of the project';
- references;
- 'appendices – technical documentation'.

The guidelines go on to list the criteria projects are required to meet to give exemption from Part I and Part II levels. At Part I the specific criteria include:

- 'the project should be of the order of 100 hours of work by each individual';
- 'the task should be to develop an IT solution to a practical problem';
- 'it should emphasise design and be documented by a technical report';
- 'the project work may be part of a group project, but the technical report and assessment must clearly identify each individual's personal contribution'.

At Part II the specific criteria include:

- 'it involves at least 150 hours of individual student effort';
- 'the task should be to develop an IT solution to a practical problem';
- 'it exhibits a structured approach to information systems practice';
- 'the product exhibits the attributes of quality, reliability, timeliness and maintainability';
- 'it must involve the production of a professional report';
- 'it must lead to a description of the process and of the product'.

The BCS documentation goes on to discuss, in more detail, requirements for projects to attain CEng and IEng accreditation. For these types of accreditation you must complete both an individual and a group project. While the criteria outlined above tend to emphasise the practical nature of projects, the individual project in this case can be either research or practically based. While the report for a practical-based project in this case should include the same components as for BCS exemption listed earlier, individual research project reports should contain in addition:

- 'a clear description of the research method used';
- 'a description of the outcome of the research'.

While the BCS maintains high standards and requirements for membership, there are many excellent projects undertaken within computer departments in universities that would not match the Society's criteria for exemption and/or accreditation. However, if you are intending to become a member of the BCS it is as well to check the level of exemption your institution holds and check that your project falls within the criteria presented here.

For more information about the BCS, and more detail on membership and exemption and accreditation, you can contact the Society directly at:

The British Computer Society
1 Sanford Street
Swindon
SN1 1HJ
UK

In addition, many academic computer departments contain a BCS 'representative' and many of your department's staff may well be members. You should ask your supervisor and other members of staff if you want to know more.

8.5 The future

8.5.1 *Your new skills*

This section discusses briefly how you will be able to apply the skills you have learnt from your project in the future. As an undergraduate you might find yourself moving on into industry or staying on within the academic community to pursue your studies further; for example, for an MPhil or PhD. As a postgraduate you may wish to remain in academia as a lecturer, a research assistant or fellow, or you too might decide to move into industry. The following points relate to a number of skills that you should have developed during the course of your project, whether at undergraduate or postgraduate level.

- *Independence.* One of the objectives of your project was to develop your skills as an independent worker. Quite often institutions refer to student projects as *Independent Studies*, which emphasises this point. Being able to work on your own without detailed supervision is certainly a skill worth cultivating and it should be one of the skills you developed during the course of your project.

  Industry expects independence from graduates, and postgraduate research degrees will require this skill as a matter of course. Be prepared to show initiative and independent thinking in your chosen career and be able to take charge of situations rather than having to be told what to do and be directed all the time.
- *Thinking.* Your project should also have taught you how to think about things more critically and in a deeper way. Independent thought and ideas represent a maturity of understanding that does not develop from merely attending lectures and tutorials. Your project should have furnished you with these kinds of skills. Once again, being able to look at things in new ways, showing deeper understanding and imagination, are skills that postgraduates are expected to have.
- *Learning.* Your project should also have taught you how to learn. As part of your project you should have had to learn new skills, new ways of looking at things and new ways of thinking. This 'learning' would not come from lectures and tutorials but from your own independent research and study. You have, therefore, understood and developed the skill of independent learning – a skill that will be useful both in industry and postgraduate work.

In addition, your project may also have provided you with an underpinning theoretical grounding in a number of areas rather than a specific technical skill. This is important as it means you can often develop and learn new skills more quickly from this firm base than you could otherwise have done by merely learning a particular tool, language or technique. For example, although you might not be able to program in a particular programming language, your underpinning theory of languages will mean that you can learn a new language very quickly. You are thus more flexible and adaptable to change than you would otherwise be with a purely technical background.

- *Technical skills.* You might also have picked up some technical skills during the course of your project. You may have learnt how to use a particular software package or apply particular analysis and design methods. While you may never use these particular technical skills again, they can provide you with a basis on which to learn similar techniques and tools in the future and they also help to bolster your CV!
- *Communication skills.* Both written and verbal communication skills are a vital part of any degree project. Improving your skills in these areas will certainly be useful, whether you go into industry or continue with postgraduate work. Verbal communication skills will be useful in industry as you will have to liaise with all kinds of people – managers, customers and clients, your own staff, consultants and so on. You might also be expected to give presentations and demonstrations and will certainly be expected to produce reports that must be clear and concise.

At postgraduate level you will encounter many new people and situations that require both your written and verbal communication skills. You might have to attend conferences or give seminars. You may be required to do some teaching or support tutorials and laboratory sessions. You will certainly have to produce written reports, transfer documents, articles and, ultimately, a thesis.

8.5.2 *Your new job*

While the above issues represent developments to your own portfolio of skills, this section looks briefly at how things might be done differently in your new career.

- *Industry.* If you go to work in industry for the first time it can be quite a culture shock. Where, in the past, you might have looked at things from a purely academic viewpoint because they interested you, within industry your primary concern will be *cost*. Work you do and projects you undertake will only be performed if they are financially viable. The

software you produce must do what it is supposed to do and what was asked for – there will be little need to justify it or place it within a wider context. You will also feel more pressure to complete work on time. Where your project was your own responsibility and you were the only one who would suffer if it was handed in late, in industry many more people will be relying on you to get the job done.
- *Higher degrees.* If you are moving from an undergraduate qualification to a postgraduate course – an MSc, MPhil or PhD – you will have to adapt your way of thinking to some extent. All specialist MScs and conversion MScs will contain a project as a significant part of their assessment. MPhils, on the other hand, are represented entirely by a research project. In both of these cases your depth of understanding and critical evaluation will have to be far more mature than at undergraduate level.

The nature of the PhD is also very much different to an undergraduate project. It will need absolute justification and contextualisation, and it will certainly have to make a contribution to knowledge. These days, timing is also more critical. Departments are penalised by funding councils if you take longer than you should to complete your PhD so pressure will be on you from other sources, not just yourself, to complete on time. You might also need to diversify your work into articles and papers for publication. As mentioned earlier, you might also have to do some teaching or help out with tutorials. An excellent book that can help you with the transition from a first degree to a PhD is Phillips and Pugh (1994), which provides some interesting information on doing a PhD.

8.6 Summary

- Although you have finished your project there are still ways in which you can continue your work further in the future: seeking funding for further research, developing commercial software from your project, seeking patents and copyright on the material you have produced, and publishing your work in academic journals.
- Your degree course and project may provide you with exemption and accreditation for membership of the British Computer Society and Engineering Council. Your own department will be able to advise you on this.
- You should have learnt a number of skills from your project that will come in useful in the future – either for a job in industry or further academic work: independence, the ability to 'think', learning skills, technical skills and communication skills.

8.7 Exercises

1. Think about how you could develop your project further in the future.
2. Find out if your course is exempt and accredited by the BCS and, if so, to what extent.
3. Write down what you have learnt by doing your project. How have you changed and developed as a result?

Bibliography

Allison, B., O'Sullivan, T., Owen, A., Rice, J., Rotherwell, A. and Saunders, C. (1996) *Research Skills for Students*, Kogan Page, London.
Bainbridge, D. (1995) *Intellectual Property*, 3rd Edition, Pitman, London.
Barnes, M. (1989) *Have Project, Will Manage*, BBC2.
Barrass, R. (1978) *Scientists Must Write: A Guide to Better Writing for Scientists, Engineers and Students*, Chapman & Hall, London.
BCS (1998) *Guidelines on Course Exemption & Accreditation*, British Computer Society, Swindon.
Belbin, M. (1993) *Team Roles at Work*, Butterworth-Heinemann, Oxford.
Bell, J. (1993) *Doing Your Research Project*, 2nd Edition, Open University Press, Buckingham.
Blaxter, L., Hughes, C. and Tight, M. (1996) *How to Research*, Open University Press, Buckingham.
Bliss, E.C. (1976) *Getting Things Done*, Futura, London.
Boehm, B.W. (1981) *Software Engineering Economics*, Prentice Hall, Englewood Cliffs, New Jersey.
Borg, W.R. and Gall, M.D. (1989) *Educational Research: An Introduction*, 5th Edition, Longman, New York.
Burcham, W.E. and Rutherford, R.J.D. (eds) (1987) *Writing Applications for Research Grants*, Educational Development Advisory Committee, Occasional Publication No. 3, University of Birmingham, UK.
Burton, C. and Michael, N. (1992) *A Practical Guide to Project Management*, Kogan Page, London.
Campbell, D. and Campbell, M. (1995) *The Student's Guide to Doing Research on the Internet*, Addison-Wesley, Wokingham.
Campbell, J.P. (1990) *Speak for Yourself: A Practical Guide to Giving Successful Presentations, Speeches and Talks*, BBC Books, London.
Collier, J.H. (ed.) (1997) *Scientific and Technical Communication*, Sage, London.
Cornford, T. and Smithson, S. (1996) *Project Research in Information Systems: A Student's Guide*, Macmillan, London.
Creme, P. and Lea, M.R. (1997) *Writing at University: A Guide for Students*, Open University Press, Buckingham.
Cryer, P. (1996) *The Research Student's Guide to Success*, Open University Press, Buckingham.
Czaja, R. and Blair, J. (1996) *Designing Surveys: A Guide to Decisions and Procedures*, Sage, London.

Dawson, C.W. and Wilby, R. (1998) 'An artificial neural network approach to rainfall-runoff modelling', *Hydrological Sciences Journal*, **43**(1), 47–66.
Day, A. (1996) *How to Get Research Published in Journals*, Gower, Aldershot.
Day, R.A. (1995) *How to Write and Publish a Scientific Paper*, 4th Edition, Cambridge University Press, Cambridge.
Easton, G. (1992) *Learning from Case Studies*, 2nd Edition, Prentice Hall, Hemel Hempstead.
Ferner, J.D. (1980) *Successful Time Management*, John Wiley and Sons, New York.
Fowler, F.J. (1995) *Improving Survey Questions: Design and Evaluation*, Sage, London.
Garratt, S. (1985) *Manage Your Time*, Fontana/Collins, London.
Gash, S. (1989) *Effective Literature Searching for Students*, Gower, Aldershot.
Gibson, H.R. (1994) *Elementary Statistics*, Wm C. Brown, Iowa.
Gill, J. and Johnson, P. (1991) *Research Methods for Managers*, Paul Chapman, London.
Goodworth, C.T. (1984) *How You Can Do More in Less Time*, Business Books, London.
Greenfield, T. (ed.) (1996) *Research Methods Guidance for Postgraduates*, Arnold, London.
Hague, P. (1993) *Questionnaire Design*, Kogan Page, London.
Haynes, M.E. (1987) *Make Every Minute Count*, Crisp Publications, Los Altos, California.
Haywood, P. and Wragg, E.C. (1982) *Evaluating the Literature*, Rediguide 2, University of Nottingham School of Education, Nottingham.
HEFCE (1998) Higher Education Funding Council for England < http://www.niss.ac.uk/education/hefc/rae2001/1_98cd.html#annc > (14 August 1998).
Helmer-Heidelberg, O. (1966) *Social Technology*, Basic Books, New York.
Herbert, M. (1990) *Planning a Research Project*, Cassell Educational, London.
Jamieson, A. (1996) *Creative Writing: Researching, Planning and Writing for Publication*, Focal, Oxford.
Jones, K. (1998) *Time Management The Essential Guide to Thinking and Working Smarter*, Marshall Publishing, London.
Kane, E. (1985) *Doing Your Own Research*, Marion Boyars, London.
Kanji, G.K. (1993) *100 Statistical Tests*, Sage, London.
Lester, J.D. (1993) *Writing Research Papers: A Complete Guide*, 7th Edition, HarperCollins, New York.
Mason, J. (1996) *Qualitative Researching*, Sage, London.
McCallum, C. (1989) *How to Write for Publication*, How To Books, Plymouth.
Melville, S. and Goddard, W. (1996) *Research Methodology: An Introduction for Science and Engineering Students*, Juta, Kenwyn, South Africa.
Morrisey, G.L. and Sechrest, T.L. (1987) *Effective Business and Technical Presentations*, 3rd Edition, Addison-Wesley, Wokingham.
Oppenheim, A.N. (1992) *Questionnaire Design, Interviewing and Attitude Measurement*, Pinter, London.
Orna, E. and Stevens, G. (1995) *Managing Information for Research*, Open University Press, Buckingham.
O'Sullivan, T., Rice, J., Rogerson, S. and Saunders, C. (1996) *Successful Group Work*, Kogan Page, London.

Phillips, E.M. and Pugh, D.S. (1994) *How to Get a PhD: A Handbook for Students and their Supervisors*, 2nd Edition, Open University Press, Buckingham.
Post, G.V. and Anderson, D.L. (1997) *Management Information Systems: Solving Business Problems with Information Technology*, Irwin, London.
Reynolds, L. and Simmonds, D. (1984) *Presentation of Data in Science*, Kluwer, Lancaster.
Ricketts, I.W. (1998) *Managing your Software Project: A Student's Guide*, Springer-Verlag, London.
Ries, J.B. and Leukefeld, C.G. (1995) *Applying For Research Funding: Getting Started and Getting Funded*, Sage, London.
Robson, C. (1993) *Real World Research*, Blackwell, Oxford.
Rogerson, S. (1989) *Project Skills Handbook*, Chartwell-Bratt, Sweden.
Rudestam, K.E. and Newton, R.R. (1992) *Surviving Your Dissertation*, Sage, London.
Saunders, M., Lewis, P. and Thornhill, A. (1997) *Research Methods for Business Students*, Pitman, London.
Sharp, J.A. and Howard, K. (1996) *The Management of a Student Research Project*, 2nd Edition, Gower, Aldershot.
Shortland, M. and Gregory, J. (1991) *Communicating Science: A Handbook*, Longman, Harlow.
Silverman, D. (ed.) (1997) *Qualitative Research Theory, Method and Practice*, Sage, London.
Smith, P. (1994) *How to Write an Assignment: Improving your Research and Presentation Skills*, How To Books, Plymouth.
Tierney, E.P. (1996) *How to Make Effective Presentations*, Sage, London.
Turla, P. and Hawkins, K.L. (1985) *Time Management Made Easy*, Panther Books, London.
Turner, J.R. (1993) *The Handbook of Project-Based Management*, McGraw-Hill, London.
University of Derby (1995) *Literature Searching for Computing*, University of Derby, internal library publication.
University of Warwick (1994) *Graduate Student Handbook 1994/95*, University of Warwick, Department of Continuing Education.
Verma, G.K. and Beard, R.M. (1981) *What is Educational Research?* Gower, Aldershot.
Weiss, J.W. and Wysocki, R.K. (1992) *5-Phase Project Management, A Practical Planning and Implementation Guide*, Addison-Wesley, Reading, Massachusetts.
Yin, R.K. (1989) *Case Study Research, Design and Methods*, Sage, London.

Index

abstracts, 114, 117–119
   example of, 118–119
academic, 1–2, 15–16, 21, 31, 34, 35, 60, 61, 131
academic advisor, 97, 98
action research, 12, 33, 35
activity networks, 41, 44–50, 102
activity-on-the-node, 44, 45
affinity diagram, 23
aims and objectives, 30, 34, 35, 38–40, 42, 83, 89, 115, 143
anti-positivism, 9
appendices, 114, 115, 139
ASLIB, 72
audience, 140, 143–154

backups, 87
BCS, *see* British Computer Society,
Belbin, 100, 101
BIDS, 72
books, 4, 22, 33, 64, 67, 68, 72–75, 77, 78, 135
brainstorming, 25, 144
British Computer Society, 69, 164–167

case study, 11–13, 16, 28, 33, 35, 88
CD-ROM, 68, 72, 87
chapter breakdown, 27, 31, 110–112
charts 119–130
   3D bar, 128, 129
   bar, 120, 121
   column, 120, 121
   combined bar, 123, 124
   histogram, 121, 122
   line, 125–128
   pie, 122, 123, 126, 127
   polar, 128, 129
   scatter diagram, 125
citing, 131–134
   Harvard, 131–137

numeric, 131, 135
Vancouver, 131, 135
clustering, 23, 27
comments, 137–139
   block, 139
   full-line, 138, 139
   in-line, 138
communication skills, 168
company, 68
   documentation, 13, 68
   reports, 13, 33, 68
computer failure, 87
conference proceedings, 68, 72, 136
contribution, 2–6, 8, 9, 11, 14, 15, 27, 30, 60, 62, 75, 76, 83, 141, 156, 157, 169
copyright, 162
critical evaluation, 13, 14, 16, 21, 35, 59, 60, 64, 75–77, 167, 169
critical reading, 76, 77
critical path, 46–48, 50

data, 3–7, 9, 12, 13, 164
data availability, 83
data continuous, 121
data presentation, 4, 119–130
deliverables, 22, 31, 34, 35
demonstrating software, 152–155
documentation, 13, 16, 137–140
documenting software, 137–140

experiment, 3, 11–13, 33

factor analysis plot, 130
figures, 113, 114, 119, 120, 124, 126
float, 49, 50
funding, 161, 162, 169

gain, 2–4, 12, 75
Gantt chart, 33, 41, 49–55, 85, 102
goal, 39, 40, 44, 89–93, 99

goals, time management, 89–93
  community, 89–93
  family, 89–93
  self, 89–93
  work, 89–93
grammar, 115–117
graphs, 4, 119–130

Harvard, 131–137
hypothesis, 12, 32, 76

ILL, *see* inter-library loans,
information, 4–7, 9, 11, 62, 65, 67–75, 119, 120
  format, 67–70
  managing, 73–75
intellectual discovery, 2, 9, 10
intellectual property rights, 162
inter-library loans, 65, 66, 69, 72, 73
Internet, 66, 69–72, 135, 136
  email, 70, 71, 103
  list servers, 71
  mailing lists, 71
  news groups, 71
IPR, see intellectual property rights,

journals, 22, 33, 64, 65, 68–72, 88, 135
justification, 1, 27, 59–61, 67, 78–80, 169

Kelvin, Lord, 28
keywords, 23, 31, 67, 71, 74
knowledge, 2–11, 14, 28, 61–63, 150, 155

Likert scale, 120
literature, 33, 59–80
literature reviews, 16, 63, 77–80, 113–116, 130
  example of, 78–80
literature search, 11, 16, 25, 59, 63, 65–72
literature surveys, 7, 21, 42, 59, 63–80, 131

manager, 97, 100, 101
managing, 82–85, 97, 102
  project, 37, 38, 82–85
  time, 42, 43, 88–96, 112
manuals, 16, 69, 137
  reference, 139, 140
  training, 139, 140
Meliorist model, 14
meta knowledge, 28

methods, 2, 3, 10–13, 16, 17
Microsoft Project, 51–55
milestones, 41, 43–47, 50, 55, 97
MPhil, 62, 68, 69, 161, 167, 169

nerves, in presentations, 149, 151, 152
numeric, 131, 135

ontology, 9
OPAC, 71, 91
oral presentations, 143–158
originality, 2, 3, 6
outcomes, 31, 34, 35

patents, 161, 162
PERT, 44
PhD, 61–63, 68, 72, 136, 155, 156, 161, 167, 169
plagiarism, 130
positivism, 9
presentation skills, 142–148, 168
  delivery, 148–150
  oral, 143–152
  written, 112, 113
priorities, 94, 95
  high, 94
  low, 94
  medium, 94
  scheduled, 94
problems, 85–88, 94–97
  dealing with, 85, 86, 94–96
  personal, 86, 87, 97
procrastination, 86, 94, 95
program, 1, 17, 134–140, 151–155, 161
programmes, TV, 69, 136
project, choosing, 21–28
project elements, 82–85
  cost, 83
  quality, 83
  resources, 83
  scope, 83
  time, 83, 88–96
project management, 37, 38, 82–85, 165
project stages, 37, 38, 84
  closure, 37, 38
  control, 37, 38, 84–85
  definition, 37–40
  inauguration, 38
  initiation, 37, 38
  planning, 33, 37–55, 90, 94
project types, 15–17
  development, 16
  evaluation, 16

176 INDEX

project types (*continued*)
   industry based, 16
   problem solving, 16
   research based, 15
proportions, 122–124, 126, 129
proposal, 38, 39
   example of, 34, 35
proposals, 28–35
   explicit, 30–35
   implicit, 29, 30
publishing, 65, 66, 161–162

qualitative analysis, 164
questionnaires, 11, 13, 88, 119, 120, 163, 164
questions handling, 150, 151, 155–158
questions in presentations, 150, 151

reading, 66, 74, 76, 77
reasoning, 9–11, 14
   deductive, 9, 10, 14
   inductive, 9–11
referencing, 70, 130–137
   ibid., 133, 134
   loc. cit., 133, 134
   op. cit., 133, 134
relevance tree, 23–25, 28, 64, 74
reports, 9, 13, 33, 60, 68, 74, 77, 78, 109–119, 156, 165, 166
   appendices, 114, 115, 165
   breakdown structure, 110–112, 116
   conclusions, 113–116
   index, 67, 114, 115
   introduction, 113–116
   structuring, 110–116
   style, 112, 113, 115, 116
research, classification, 10–14
   approach, 11
   field, 11
   nature, 11
research, good, 13, 14
research methods, 11–13, 33–35, 76, 77, 166
   action research, 12, 16
   case study, 11–13, 16
   experiment, 11–13
   survey, 11–13
research process, 6–9, 11
   circulatory, 6–8
   evolutionary, 6, 8
   generalised, 6, 7
   sequential, 6, 7
research symmetry, 32
research territory map, 23, 25, 28, 74

resource requirements, 33, 83, 96
rolling wave planning, 54, 55
RTM, *see* research territory map,

sampling, 12, 76
scheduling, 41, 49–53
slack, 49, 50
so what? test, 27, 32
spider diagrams, 23, 25, 26, 28
stubs, 155
studies, 11–13
   causal, 12
   cross-sectional, 13
   descriptive, 11
   explanatory, 11
   exploratory, 11
   longitudinal, 13
supervisor, 17, 38, 83, 96–99
   using, 96–99
   choosing, 35, 36
   academic advisor, 97, 98
   manager, 97, 98
survey, 7, 11–13, 33, 121, 122, 163, 164
SWOT analysis, 101

tables, 114, 119, 120, 126
teams, 99–103
   work roles, 100, 101
technical skills, 101, 102
theory, 3, 5, 7, 11
theses, 68, 69, 72, 136, 168
time, 83, 88–96, 112
   categories of, 92–94
   essential, 88, 93
   serviceable, 88, 93
time log, 90, 91, 93
time management, 88–96, 112
topics, selection of, 22, 23, 25, 27, 29

ULRICHS, 72
user guides, 137, 139, 140

visual aids, 143, 144, 146–148
viva voce examinations, 155–158

WBS, *see* work breakdown structure
weakening, 85, 86, 88, 97
wisdom, 4–6, 10, 13, 14
work breakdown structure, 41–44
writing, 109–119
   approaches to, 110–112
   order of, 112–114
   style, 115, 116
   top-down, 110–112